The

If you accept my words and store up
my commands within you... and if you
look for it as for silver and search for
it as for hidden treasure, then you will
understand the fear of the LORD and
find the knowledge of God.

Proverbs 2:1,4–5

NIV
Adventure BIBLE
Field Notes
Psalms

My First Bible Journal

Features written by
Lawrence O. Richards

Contents

Preface to the
New International Version

The goal of the New International Version (NIV) is to enable English-speaking people from around the world to read and hear God's eternal Word in their own language. Our work as translators is motivated by our conviction that the Bible is God's Word in written form. We believe that the Bible contains the divine answer to the deepest needs of humanity, sheds unique light on our path in a dark world and sets forth the way to our eternal well-being. Out of these deep convictions, we have sought to recreate as far as possible the experience of the original audience — blending transparency to the original text with accessibility for the millions of English speakers around the world. We have prioritized accuracy, clarity and literary quality with the goal of creating a translation suitable for public and private reading, evangelism, teaching, preaching, memorizing and liturgical use. We have also sought to preserve a measure of continuity with the long tradition of translating the Scriptures into English.

The complete NIV Bible was first published in 1978. It was a completely new translation made by over a hundred scholars working directly from the best available Hebrew, Aramaic and Greek texts. The translators came from the United States, Great Britain, Canada, Australia and New Zealand, giving the translation an international scope. They were from many denominations and churches — including Anglican, Assemblies of God, Baptist, Brethren, Christian Reformed, Church of Christ, Evangelical Covenant, Evangelical Free, Lutheran, Mennonite, Methodist, Nazarene, Presbyterian, Wesleyan and others. This breadth of denominational and theological perspective helped to safeguard the translation from sectarian bias. For these reasons, and by the grace of God, the NIV has gained a wide readership in all parts of the English-speaking world.

The work of translating the Bible is never finished. As good as they are, English translations must be regularly updated so that they will continue to communicate accurately the meaning of God's Word. Updates are needed in order to reflect the latest developments in our understanding of the biblical world and its languages and to keep pace with changes in English usage. Recognizing, then, that the NIV would retain its ability to communicate God's Word accurately only if it were regularly updated, the original translators established the Committee on Bible Translation (CBT). The Committee is a self-perpetuating group of biblical scholars charged with keeping abreast of advances in biblical scholarship and changes in English and issuing periodic updates to the NIV. The CBT is an independent, self-governing body and has sole responsibility for the NIV text. The Committee mirrors the original group of translators in its diverse international and denominational makeup and in its unifying commitment to the Bible as God's inspired Word.

In obedience to its mandate, the Committee has issued periodic updates to the NIV. An initial revision was released in 1984. A more thorough revision process was completed in 2005, resulting in the separately published TNIV. The updated NIV you now have in your hands builds on both the original NIV and the TNIV and represents the latest effort of the Committee to articulate God's unchanging Word in the way the original authors might have said it had they been speaking in English to the global English-speaking audience today.

Translation Philosophy

The Committee's translating work has been governed by three widely accepted principles about the way people use words and about the way we understand them.

First, the meaning of words is determined by the way that users of the language actually use them at any given time. For the biblical languages, therefore, the Committee utilizes the best and most recent scholarship on the way Hebrew, Aramaic and Greek words were being used in biblical times. At the same time, the Committee carefully studies the state of modern English. Good translation is like good communication: one must know the target audience so that the appropriate choices can be made about which English words to use to represent the original words of Scripture. From its inception, the NIV has had as its target the general English-speaking population all over the world, the "International" in its title reflecting this concern. The aim of the Committee is to put the Scriptures into natural English that will communicate effectively with the broadest possible audience of English speakers.

Modern technology has enhanced the Committee's ability to choose the right English words to convey the meaning of the original text. The field of computational linguistics harnesses the power of computers to provide broadly applicable and current data about the state of the language. Translators can now access huge databases of modern English to better understand the current meaning and usage of key words. The Committee utilized this resource in preparing the 2011 edition of the NIV. An area of especially rapid and significant change in English is the way certain nouns and pronouns are used to refer to human beings. The Committee therefore requested experts in computational linguistics at Collins Dictionaries to pose some key questions about this usage to its database of English — the largest in the world, with over 4.4 billion words, gathered from several English-speaking countries and including both spoken and written English. (The Collins Study, called "The Development and Use of Gender Language in Contemporary English," can be accessed at *http://www.thenivbible.com/about-the-niv/about-the-2011-edition/*.) The study revealed that the most popular words to describe the human race in modern U.S. English were "humanity," "man" and "mankind." The Committee then used this data in the updated NIV, choosing from among these three words (and occasionally others also) depending on the context.

A related issue creates a larger problem for modern translations: the move away from using the third-person masculine singular pronouns — "he/him/his" — to refer to men and women equally. This usage does persist in some forms of English, and this revision therefore occasionally uses these pronouns in a generic sense. But the tendency, recognized in day-to-day usage and confirmed by the Collins study, is away from the generic use of "he," "him" and "his." In recognition of this shift in language and in an effort to translate into the natural English that people are actually using, this revision of the NIV generally uses other constructions when the biblical text is plainly addressed to men and women equally. The reader will encounter especially frequently a "they," "their" or "them" to express a generic singular idea. Thus, for instance, Mark 8:36 reads: "What good is it for someone to gain the whole world, yet forfeit their soul?" This generic use of the "distributive" or "singular" "they/them/their" has been used for many centuries by respected writers of English and has now become established as standard English, spoken and written, all over the world.

A second linguistic principle that feeds into the Committee's translation work is that meaning is found not in individual words, as vital as they are, but in larger clusters: phrases, clauses, sentences, discourses. Translation is not, as many people think, a matter of word substitution: English word *x* in place of Hebrew word *y*. Translators must first determine the meaning of the words of the biblical languages in the context of the passage and then select English words that accurately communicate that meaning to modern listeners and readers. This means that accurate translation will not always reflect the exact structure of the original language. To be sure, there is debate over the degree to which translators should try to preserve the "form" of the original text in English. From the beginning, the NIV has taken a mediating position on this issue. The manual produced when the translation that became the NIV was first being planned states: "If the Greek or Hebrew syntax has a good parallel in modern English, it should be used. But if there is no good parallel, the English syntax appropriate to the meaning of the original is to be chosen." It is fine, in other words, to carry over the form of the biblical languages into English — but not at the expense of natural expression. The principle that meaning resides in larger clusters of words means that the Committee has not insisted on a "word-for-word" approach to translation. We certainly believe that every word of Scripture is inspired by God and therefore to be carefully studied to determine what God is saying to us. It is for this reason that the Committee labors over every single word of the original texts, working hard to determine how each of those words contributes to what the text is saying. Ultimately, however, it is how these individual words function in combination with other words that determines meaning.

A third linguistic principle guiding the Committee in its translation work is the recognition that words have a spectrum of meaning. It is popular to define a word by using another word, or "gloss," to substitute for it. This substitute word is then sometimes called the "literal" meaning of a word. In fact, however, words have a range of possible meanings. Those meanings will vary depending on the context, and words in one language will usually not occupy the same semantic range as words in another language. The Committee therefore studies each original word of Scripture in its context to identify its meaning in a particular verse and then chooses an appropriate English word (or phrase) to represent it. It is impossible, then, to translate any given Hebrew, Aramaic or Greek word with the same English word all the time. The Committee does try to translate related occurrences of a word in the original languages with the same English word in order to preserve the connection for the English reader. But the Committee generally privileges clear natural meaning over a concern with consistency in rendering particular words.

Textual Basis

For the Old Testament the standard Hebrew text, the Masoretic Text as published in the latest edition of *Biblia Hebraica*, has been used throughout. The Masoretic Text tradition contains marginal notations that offer variant readings. These have sometimes been followed instead of the text itself. Because such instances involve variants within the Masoretic tradition, they have not been indicated in the textual notes. In a few cases, words in the basic consonantal text have been divided differently than in the Masoretic Text. Such cases are usually indicated in the textual footnotes. The Dead Sea Scrolls contain biblical texts that represent an earlier stage of the transmission of the Hebrew text. They have been consulted, as have been the Samaritan Pentateuch and the ancient scribal traditions concerning deliberate textual changes. The translators also consulted the more important early versions. Readings from these versions, the Dead Sea Scrolls and the scribal traditions were occasionally followed where the Masoretic Text seemed doubtful and where accepted principles of textual criticism showed that one or more of these textual witnesses appeared to provide the correct reading. In rare cases, the translators have emended the Hebrew text where it appears to have become corrupted at an even earlier stage of its transmission. These departures from the Masoretic Text are also indicated in the textual footnotes. Sometimes the vowel indicators (which are later additions to the basic consonantal text) found in the Masoretic Text did not, in the judgment of the translators, represent the correct vowels for the original text. Accordingly, some words have been read with a different set of vowels. These instances are usually not indicated in the footnotes.

The Greek text used in translating the New Testament has been an eclectic one, based on the latest editions of the Nestle-Aland/United Bible Societies' Greek New Testament. The translators have made their choices among the variant readings in accordance with widely accepted principles of New Testament textual criticism. Footnotes call attention to places where uncertainty remains.

The New Testament authors, writing in Greek, often quote the Old Testament from its ancient Greek version, the Septuagint. This is one reason why some of the Old Testament quotations in the NIV New Testament are not identical to the corresponding passages in the NIV Old Testament. Such quotations in the New Testament are indicated with the footnote "(see Septuagint)."

Footnotes and Formatting

Footnotes in this version are of several kinds, most of which need no explanation. Those giving alternative translations begin with "Or" and generally introduce the alternative with the last word preceding it in the text, except when it is a single-word alternative. When poetry is quoted in a footnote a slash mark indicates a line division.

It should be noted that references to diseases, minerals, flora and fauna, architectural details, clothing, jewelry, musical instruments and other articles cannot always be identified with precision. Also, linear measurements and measures of capacity can only be approximated (see the Table of Weights and Measures). Although *Selah*, used mainly in the Psalms, is probably a musical term, its meaning is uncertain. Since it may interrupt reading and distract the reader, this word has not been kept in the English text, but every occurrence has been signaled by a footnote.

As an aid to the reader, sectional headings have been inserted. They are not to be regarded as part of the biblical text and are not intended for oral reading. It is the Committee's hope that these headings may prove more helpful to the reader than the traditional chapter divisions, which were introduced long after the Bible was written.

Sometimes the chapter and/or verse numbering in English translations of the Old Testament differs from that found in published Hebrew texts. This is particularly the case in the Psalms, where the traditional titles are included in the Hebrew verse numbering. Such differences are indicated in the footnotes at the bottom of the page. In the New Testament, verse numbers that marked off portions of the traditional English text not supported by the best Greek manuscripts now appear in brackets, with a footnote indicating the text that has been omitted (see, for example, Matthew 17:[21]).

Mark 16:9 – 20 and John 7:53 — 8:11, although long accorded virtually equal status with the rest of the Gospels in which they stand, have a questionable standing in the textual history of the New Testament, as noted in the bracketed annotations with which they are set off. A different typeface has been chosen for these passages to indicate their uncertain status.

Basic formatting of the text, such as lining the poetry, paragraphing (both prose and poetry), setting up of (administrative-like) lists, indenting letters and lengthy prayers within narratives and the insertion of sectional headings, has been the work of the Committee. However, the choice between single-column and double-column formats has been left to the publishers. Also the issuing of "red-letter" editions is a publisher's choice — one that the Committee does not endorse.

The Committee has again been reminded that every human effort is flawed — including this revision of the NIV. We trust, however, that many will find in it an improved representation of the Word of God, through which they hear his call to faith in our Lord Jesus Christ and to service in his kingdom. We offer this version of the Bible to him in whose name and for whose glory it has been made.

The Committee on Bible Translation

Who wrote this book?

David wrote 73 of the 150 psalms. Several different people wrote the others.

Why was this book written?

The psalms show God's people how to talk to him and to worship him.

What kinds of psalms are there?

There are seven kinds of psalms:

1. *Praise psalms* like Psalms 33 and 103 show us how to thank God for who he is.
2. *History psalms* like Psalms 68 and 106 tell what God has done for his people.
3. *Friendship psalms* like Psalms 8 and 23 remind us that God loves us and tell us how we can show our love to him.
4. *Anger psalms* like Psalms 35 and 137 ask God to punish evil people.
5. *Confession psalms* like Psalms 32 and 51 show how to talk to God about our sins.
6. *Messiah psalms* like Psalms 22 and 89 tell us about Jesus.
7. *Worship psalms* like Psalms 30 and 122 were used on special religious holidays to worship God with other people.

What kind of poetry is used in this book?

The psalms do not rhyme. Hebrew poetry repeats ideas instead of repeating sounds.

When were the psalms written?

The psalms were probably written between about 1400 and 500 BC.

What are some favorite psalms?

God's creation and Word	Psalm 19
God is our shepherd	Psalm 23
Confessing sin to God	Psalm 32
Trusting God	Psalm 37
Don't be jealous	Psalm 73
God's great love	Psalm 89
How great God is	Psalm 104
Loving God's Word	Psalm 119

BOOK I

Psalms 1 – 41

Psalm 1

1 Blessed is the one
    who does not walk in step with the wicked
  or stand in the way that sinners take
    or sit in the company of mockers,
2 but whose delight is in the law of the LORD,
    and who meditates on his law day and night.
3 That person is like a tree planted by streams of water,
    which yields its fruit in season
  and whose leaf does not wither —
    whatever they do prospers.

4 Not so the wicked!
    They are like chaff
    that the wind blows away.
5 Therefore the wicked will not stand in the judgment,
    nor sinners in the assembly of the righteous.

6 For the LORD watches over the way of the righteous,
    but the way of the wicked leads to destruction.

Psalm 2

1 Why do the nations conspire[a]
    and the peoples plot in vain?
2 The kings of the earth rise up
    and the rulers band together
    against the LORD and against his anointed, saying,
3 "Let us break their chains
    and throw off their shackles."

4 The One enthroned in heaven laughs;
    the Lord scoffs at them.
5 He rebukes them in his anger
    and terrifies them in his wrath, saying,
6 "I have installed my king
    on Zion, my holy mountain."

7 I will proclaim the LORD's decree:

He said to me, "You are my son;
    today I have become your father.

---

a 1 Hebrew; Septuagint *rage*

⁸Ask me,
    and I will make the nations your inheritance,
    the ends of the earth your possession.
⁹You will break them with a rod of iron*ᵃ*;
    you will dash them to pieces like pottery."

¹⁰Therefore, you kings, be wise;
    be warned, you rulers of the earth.
¹¹Serve the Lord with fear
    and celebrate his rule with trembling.
¹²Kiss his son, or he will be angry
    and your way will lead to your destruction,
  for his wrath can flare up in a moment.
    Blessed are all who take refuge in him.

Psalm 3ᵇ

A psalm of David. When he fled from his son Absalom.

¹Lord, how many are my foes!
    How many rise up against me!
²Many are saying of me,
    "God will not deliver him."ᶜ

³But you, Lord, are a shield around me,
    my glory, the One who lifts my head high.
⁴I call out to the Lord,
    and he answers me from his holy mountain.

⁵I lie down and sleep;
    I wake again, because the Lord sustains me.
⁶I will not fear though tens of thousands
    assail me on every side.

⁷Arise, Lord!
    Deliver me, my God!
  Strike all my enemies on the jaw;
    break the teeth of the wicked.

⁸From the Lord comes deliverance.
    May your blessing be on your people.

Psalm 4ᵈ

For the director of music. With stringed instruments. A psalm of David.

¹Answer me when I call to you,
    my righteous God.
  Give me relief from my distress;
    have mercy on me and hear my prayer.

ᵃ 9 Or *will rule them with an iron scepter* (see Septuagint and Syriac)   ᵇ In Hebrew texts 3:1-8 is numbered 3:2-9.   ᶜ 2 The Hebrew has *Selah* (a word of uncertain meaning) here and at the end of verses 4 and 8.   ᵈ In Hebrew texts 4:1-8 is numbered 4:2-9.

Safe at Night

David was running from an enemy army when he wrote this psalm. You can read the story in 2 Samuel 15:10–14. Now read Psalm 3. Verses 1 and 2 tell how David felt. Verses 3 and 4 tell what David remembered about God. Verses 5 and 6 tell how David was able to sleep, even when he was in danger. Verses 7 and 8 tell what David prayed.

Here's something to help you if you are afraid at night. Cut a shield from a piece of cardboard. Cover it with blue construction paper. Tape on two strips of aluminum foil in the shape of a cross. Put the shield under your pillow at night to remind you that God will guard you, just as he guarded King David.

Psalm 3:1–8

² How long will you people turn my glory into shame?
   How long will you love delusions and seek false gods^a?^b
³ Know that the LORD has set apart his faithful servant for himself;
   the LORD hears when I call to him.

⁴ Tremble and^c do not sin;
   when you are on your beds,
   search your hearts and be silent.
⁵ Offer the sacrifices of the righteous
   and trust in the LORD.

⁶ Many, LORD, are asking, "Who will bring us prosperity?"
   Let the light of your face shine on us.
⁷ Fill my heart with joy
   when their grain and new wine abound.

⁸ In peace I will lie down and sleep,
   for you alone, LORD,
   make me dwell in safety.

Psalm 5^d

For the director of music. For pipes. A psalm of David.

¹ Listen to my words, LORD,
   consider my lament.
² Hear my cry for help,
   my King and my God,
   for to you I pray.

³ In the morning, LORD, you hear my voice;
   in the morning I lay my requests before you
   and wait expectantly.
⁴ For you are not a God who is pleased with wickedness;
   with you, evil people are not welcome.
⁵ The arrogant cannot stand
   in your presence.
 You hate all who do wrong;
⁶   you destroy those who tell lies.
 The bloodthirsty and deceitful
   you, LORD, detest.
⁷ But I, by your great love,
   can come into your house;
 in reverence I bow down
   toward your holy temple.

⁸ Lead me, LORD, in your righteousness
   because of my enemies —
   make your way straight before me.

---

^a 2 Or *seek lies*   ^b 2 The Hebrew has *Selah* (a word of uncertain meaning) here and at the end of verse 4.
^c 4 Or *In your anger* (see Septuagint)   ^d In Hebrew texts 5:1-12 is numbered 5:2-13.

⁹ Not a word from their mouth can be trusted;
    their heart is filled with malice.
  Their throat is an open grave;
    with their tongues they tell lies.
¹⁰ Declare them guilty, O God!
    Let their intrigues be their downfall.
  Banish them for their many sins,
    for they have rebelled against you.
¹¹ But let all who take refuge in you be glad;
    let them ever sing for joy.
  Spread your protection over them,
    that those who love your name may rejoice in you.

¹² Surely, LORD, you bless the righteous;
    you surround them with your favor as with a shield.

Psalm 6ᵃ

For the director of music. With stringed instruments.
According to sheminith.ᵇ A psalm of David.

¹ LORD, do not rebuke me in your anger
    or discipline me in your wrath.
² Have mercy on me, LORD, for I am faint;
    heal me, LORD, for my bones are in agony.
³ My soul is in deep anguish.
    How long, LORD, how long?

⁴ Turn, LORD, and deliver me;
    save me because of your unfailing love.
⁵ Among the dead no one proclaims your name.
    Who praises you from the grave?

⁶ I am worn out from my groaning.

  All night long I flood my bed with weeping
    and drench my couch with tears.
⁷ My eyes grow weak with sorrow;
    they fail because of all my foes.

⁸ Away from me, all you who do evil,
    for the LORD has heard my weeping.
⁹ The LORD has heard my cry for mercy;
    the LORD accepts my prayer.
¹⁰ All my enemies will be overwhelmed with shame and anguish;
    they will turn back and suddenly be put to shame.

ᵃ In Hebrew texts 6:1-10 is numbered 6:2-11.   ᵇ Title: Probably a musical term

Psalm 7[a]

A shiggaion[b] of David, which he sang to the LORD *concerning Cush, a Benjamite.*

¹ LORD my God, I take refuge in you;
    save and deliver me from all who pursue me,
² or they will tear me apart like a lion
    and rip me to pieces with no one to rescue me.

³ LORD my God, if I have done this
    and there is guilt on my hands —
⁴ if I have repaid my ally with evil
    or without cause have robbed my foe —
⁵ then let my enemy pursue and overtake me;
    let him trample my life to the ground
    and make me sleep in the dust.[c]

⁶ Arise, LORD, in your anger;
    rise up against the rage of my enemies.
    Awake, my God; decree justice.
⁷ Let the assembled peoples gather around you,
    while you sit enthroned over them on high.
⁸   Let the LORD judge the peoples.
  Vindicate me, LORD, according to my righteousness,
    according to my integrity, O Most High.
⁹ Bring to an end the violence of the wicked
    and make the righteous secure —
  you, the righteous God
    who probes minds and hearts.

¹⁰ My shield[d] is God Most High,
    who saves the upright in heart.
¹¹ God is a righteous judge,
    a God who displays his wrath every day.
¹² If he does not relent,
    he[e] will sharpen his sword;
    he will bend and string his bow.
¹³ He has prepared his deadly weapons;
    he makes ready his flaming arrows.

¹⁴ Whoever is pregnant with evil
    conceives trouble and gives birth to disillusionment.
¹⁵ Whoever digs a hole and scoops it out
    falls into the pit they have made.
¹⁶ The trouble they cause recoils on them;
    their violence comes down on their own heads.

¹⁷ I will give thanks to the LORD because of his righteousness;
    I will sing the praises of the name of the LORD Most High.

---

[a] In Hebrew texts 7:1-17 is numbered 7:2-18.   [b] Title: Probably a literary or musical term   [c] 5 The Hebrew has
Selah (a word of uncertain meaning) here.   [d] 10 Or *sovereign*   [e] 12 Or *If anyone does not repent, / God*

Life in Bible Times

What God Is Like

Psalm 7:10 says that God is like a shield. A shield protected a soldier from the spears and arrows of his enemies. To call God a shield means that God will protect the person who trusts him.

Psalm 8[a]

For the director of music. According to gittith.[b] A psalm of David.

[1] LORD, our Lord,
  how majestic is your name in all the earth!

 You have set your glory
  in the heavens.
[2] Through the praise of children and infants
  you have established a stronghold against your enemies,
  to silence the foe and the avenger.
[3] When I consider your heavens,
  the work of your fingers,
 the moon and the stars,
  which you have set in place,
[4] what is mankind that you are mindful of them,
  human beings that you care for them?[c]

[5] You have made them[d] a little lower than the angels[e]
  and crowned them[d] with glory and honor.
[6] You made them rulers over the works of your hands;
  you put everything under their[f] feet:
[7] all flocks and herds,
  and the animals of the wild,
[8] the birds in the sky,
  and the fish in the sea,
  all that swim the paths of the seas.

[9] LORD, our Lord,
  how majestic is your name in all the earth!

Psalm 9[g,h]

For the director of music. To the tune of "The Death of the Son." A psalm of David.

[1] I will give thanks to you, LORD, with all my heart;
  I will tell of all your wonderful deeds.
[2] I will be glad and rejoice in you;
  I will sing the praises of your name, O Most High.

[3] My enemies turn back;
  they stumble and perish before you.
[4] For you have upheld my right and my cause,
  sitting enthroned as the righteous judge.
[5] You have rebuked the nations and destroyed the wicked;
  you have blotted out their name for ever and ever.

[a] In Hebrew texts 8:1-9 is numbered 8:2-10.   [b] Title: Probably a musical term   [c] 4 Or *what is a human being that you are mindful of him, / a son of man that you care for him?*   [d] 5 Or *him*   [e] 5 Or *than God*   [f] 6 Or *made him ruler . . . ; / . . . his*   [g] Psalms 9 and 10 may originally have been a single acrostic poem in which alternating lines began with the successive letters of the Hebrew alphabet. In the Septuagint they constitute one psalm.   [h] In Hebrew texts 9:1-20 is numbered 9:2-21.

Look at the Heavens

David often slept outside at night when he cared for his father's sheep. He watched the moon and the stars and thought about God. Read Psalm 8 and see what David thought when he looked up.

Some clear night go outside and look at the stars. Without a telescope you can see just over 1,000 stars. If you had looked through the first telescope, made many years ago by Galileo, you would have seen over 3,000. With today's big telescopes you can see millions of stars in the sky! It's good to lie on your back, look at the stars, and think about how great God is. In the space below, write down one thing you wonder about God.

Psalm 8:1-5

⁶ Endless ruin has overtaken my enemies,
  you have uprooted their cities;
  even the memory of them has perished.

⁷ The LORD reigns forever;
  he has established his throne for judgment.
⁸ He rules the world in righteousness
  and judges the peoples with equity.
⁹ The LORD is a refuge for the oppressed,
  a stronghold in times of trouble.
¹⁰ Those who know your name trust in you,
  for you, LORD, have never forsaken those who seek you.

¹¹ Sing the praises of the LORD, enthroned in Zion;
  proclaim among the nations what he has done.
¹² For he who avenges blood remembers;
  he does not ignore the cries of the afflicted.

¹³ LORD, see how my enemies persecute me!
  Have mercy and lift me up from the gates of death,
¹⁴ that I may declare your praises
  in the gates of Daughter Zion,
  and there rejoice in your salvation.

¹⁵ The nations have fallen into the pit they have dug;
  their feet are caught in the net they have hidden.
¹⁶ The LORD is known by his acts of justice;
  the wicked are ensnared by the work of their hands.[a]
¹⁷ The wicked go down to the realm of the dead,
  all the nations that forget God.
¹⁸ But God will never forget the needy;
  the hope of the afflicted will never perish.

¹⁹ Arise, LORD, do not let mortals triumph;
  let the nations be judged in your presence.
²⁰ Strike them with terror, LORD;
  let the nations know they are only mortal.

Psalm 10[b]

¹ Why, LORD, do you stand far off?
  Why do you hide yourself in times of trouble?

² In his arrogance the wicked man hunts down the weak,
  who are caught in the schemes he devises.
³ He boasts about the cravings of his heart;
  he blesses the greedy and reviles the LORD.
⁴ In his pride the wicked man does not seek him;
  in all his thoughts there is no room for God.

---

[a] 16 The Hebrew has *Higgaion* and *Selah* (words of uncertain meaning) here; *Selah* occurs also at the end of verse 20.   [b] Psalms 9 and 10 may originally have been a single acrostic poem in which alternating lines began with the successive letters of the Hebrew alphabet. In the Septuagint they constitute one psalm.

_____

_____

_____

_____

_____

_____

_____

_____

_____

_____

_____

_____

_____

_____

_____

Life in Bible Times

What God Is Like

Psalm 9:7 says that God is like a king on heaven's throne. In Bible times a king sat on his throne to give orders and make decisions. To say that God is a king on heaven's throne means that what he commands will happen.

⁵His ways are always prosperous;
   your laws are rejected byᵃ him;
   he sneers at all his enemies.
⁶He says to himself, "Nothing will ever shake me."
   He swears, "No one will ever do me harm."

⁷His mouth is full of lies and threats;
   trouble and evil are under his tongue.
⁸He lies in wait near the villages;
   from ambush he murders the innocent.
 His eyes watch in secret for his victims;
⁹   like a lion in cover he lies in wait.
 He lies in wait to catch the helpless;
   he catches the helpless and drags them off in his net.
¹⁰His victims are crushed, they collapse;
   they fall under his strength.
¹¹He says to himself, "God will never notice;
   he covers his face and never sees."

¹²Arise, LORD! Lift up your hand, O God.
   Do not forget the helpless.
¹³Why does the wicked man revile God?
   Why does he say to himself,
   "He won't call me to account"?
¹⁴But you, God, see the trouble of the afflicted;
   you consider their grief and take it in hand.
 The victims commit themselves to you;
   you are the helper of the fatherless.
¹⁵Break the arm of the wicked man;
   call the evildoer to account for his wickedness
   that would not otherwise be found out.

¹⁶The LORD is King for ever and ever;
   the nations will perish from his land.
¹⁷You, LORD, hear the desire of the afflicted;
   you encourage them, and you listen to their cry,
¹⁸defending the fatherless and the oppressed,
   so that mere earthly mortals
   will never again strike terror.

Psalm 11

For the director of music. Of David.

¹In the LORD I take refuge.
   How then can you say to me:
   "Flee like a bird to your mountain.
²For look, the wicked bend their bows;
   they set their arrows against the strings

ᵃ 5 See Septuagint; Hebrew / *they are haughty, and your laws are far from*

to shoot from the shadows
   at the upright in heart.
³ When the foundations are being destroyed,
   what can the righteous do?"

⁴ The LORD is in his holy temple;
   the LORD is on his heavenly throne.
He observes everyone on earth;
   his eyes examine them.
⁵ The LORD examines the righteous,
   but the wicked, those who love violence,
   he hates with a passion.
⁶ On the wicked he will rain
   fiery coals and burning sulfur;
   a scorching wind will be their lot.

⁷ For the LORD is righteous,
   he loves justice;
   the upright will see his face.

Psalm 12ᵃ

For the director of music. According to sheminith.ᵇ *A psalm of David.*

¹ Help, LORD, for no one is faithful anymore;
   those who are loyal have vanished from the human race.
² Everyone lies to their neighbor;
   they flatter with their lips
   but harbor deception in their hearts.

³ May the LORD silence all flattering lips
   and every boastful tongue —
⁴ those who say,
   "By our tongues we will prevail;
   our own lips will defend us — who is lord over us?"

⁵ "Because the poor are plundered and the needy groan,
   I will now arise," says the LORD.
   "I will protect them from those who malign them."
⁶ And the words of the LORD are flawless,
   like silver purified in a crucible,
   like goldᶜ refined seven times.

⁷ You, LORD, will keep the needy safe
   and will protect us forever from the wicked,
⁸ who freely strut about
   when what is vile is honored by the human race.

ᵃ In Hebrew texts 12:1-8 is numbered 12:2-9.   ᵇ Title: Probably a musical term   ᶜ 6 Probable reading of the original Hebrew text; Masoretic Text *earth*

Psalm 13[a]

For the director of music. A psalm of David.

¹How long, L<small>ORD</small>? Will you forget me forever?
　　How long will you hide your face from me?
²How long must I wrestle with my thoughts
　　and day after day have sorrow in my heart?
　　How long will my enemy triumph over me?

³Look on me and answer, L<small>ORD</small> my God.
　　Give light to my eyes, or I will sleep in death,
⁴and my enemy will say, "I have overcome him,"
　　and my foes will rejoice when I fall.

⁵But I trust in your unfailing love;
　　my heart rejoices in your salvation.
⁶I will sing the L<small>ORD</small>'s praise,
　　for he has been good to me.

Psalm 14

For the director of music. Of David.

¹The fool[b] says in his heart,
　　"There is no God."
They are corrupt, their deeds are vile;
　　there is no one who does good.

²The L<small>ORD</small> looks down from heaven
　　on all mankind
to see if there are any who understand,
　　any who seek God.
³All have turned away, all have become corrupt;
　　there is no one who does good,
　　not even one.

⁴Do all these evildoers know nothing?

They devour my people as though eating bread;
　　they never call on the L<small>ORD</small>.
⁵But there they are, overwhelmed with dread,
　　for God is present in the company of the righteous.
⁶You evildoers frustrate the plans of the poor,
　　but the L<small>ORD</small> is their refuge.

⁷Oh, that salvation for Israel would come out of Zion!
　　When the L<small>ORD</small> restores his people,
　　let Jacob rejoice and Israel be glad!

---

[a] In Hebrew texts 13:1-6 is numbered 13:2-6.　　[b] *1* The Hebrew words rendered *fool* in Psalms denote one who is morally deficient.

Psalm 15

A psalm of David.

[1] LORD, who may dwell in your sacred tent?
    Who may live on your holy mountain?

[2] The one whose walk is blameless,
    who does what is righteous,
    who speaks the truth from their heart;
[3] whose tongue utters no slander,
    who does no wrong to a neighbor,
    and casts no slur on others;
[4] who despises a vile person
    but honors those who fear the LORD;
  who keeps an oath even when it hurts,
    and does not change their mind;
[5] who lends money to the poor without interest;
    who does not accept a bribe against the innocent.

Whoever does these things
    will never be shaken.

Psalm 16

A miktam[a] of David.

[1] Keep me safe, my God,
    for in you I take refuge.

[2] I say to the LORD, "You are my Lord;
    apart from you I have no good thing."
[3] I say of the holy people who are in the land,
    "They are the noble ones in whom is all my delight."
[4] Those who run after other gods will suffer more and more.
    I will not pour out libations of blood to such gods
    or take up their names on my lips.

[5] LORD, you alone are my portion and my cup;
    you make my lot secure.
[6] The boundary lines have fallen for me in pleasant places;
    surely I have a delightful inheritance.
[7] I will praise the LORD, who counsels me;
    even at night my heart instructs me.
[8] I keep my eyes always on the LORD.
    With him at my right hand, I will not be shaken.

[9] Therefore my heart is glad and my tongue rejoices;
    my body also will rest secure,
[10] because you will not abandon me to the realm of the dead,
    nor will you let your faithful[b] one see decay.

[a] Title: Probably a literary or musical term   [b] 10 Or *holy*

[11] You make known to me the path of life;
   you will fill me with joy in your presence,
   with eternal pleasures at your right hand.

Psalm 17

A prayer of David.

[1] Hear me, LORD, my plea is just;
   listen to my cry.
 Hear my prayer—
   it does not rise from deceitful lips.
[2] Let my vindication come from you;
   may your eyes see what is right.

[3] Though you probe my heart,
   though you examine me at night and test me,
 you will find that I have planned no evil;
   my mouth has not transgressed.
[4] Though people tried to bribe me,
   I have kept myself from the ways of the violent
   through what your lips have commanded.
[5] My steps have held to your paths;
   my feet have not stumbled.

[6] I call on you, my God, for you will answer me;
   turn your ear to me and hear my prayer.
[7] Show me the wonders of your great love,
   you who save by your right hand
   those who take refuge in you from their foes.
[8] Keep me as the apple of your eye;
   hide me in the shadow of your wings
[9] from the wicked who are out to destroy me,
   from my mortal enemies who surround me.

[10] They close up their callous hearts,
   and their mouths speak with arrogance.
[11] They have tracked me down, they now surround me,
   with eyes alert, to throw me to the ground.
[12] They are like a lion hungry for prey,
   like a fierce lion crouching in cover.

[13] Rise up, LORD, confront them, bring them down;
   with your sword rescue me from the wicked.
[14] By your hand save me from such people, LORD,
   from those of this world whose reward is in this life.
 May what you have stored up for the wicked fill their bellies;
   may their children gorge themselves on it,
   and may there be leftovers for their little ones.

[15] As for me, I will be vindicated and will see your face;
   when I awake, I will be satisfied with seeing your likeness.

_____

_____

_____

_____

_____

_____

_____

_____

_____

_____

_____

_____

_____

_____

_____

_____

_____

_____

Life in Bible Times

What God Is Like

Psalm 17:13 says that God is like a warrior. He protects us and comes to our rescue when we are in trouble.

When others threaten to hurt us and we feel scared and helpless, it is good to remember that God is on our side.

Psalm 18[a]

For the director of music. Of David the servant of the LORD.
He sang to the LORD the words of this song when the
LORD delivered him from the hand of all his enemies
and from the hand of Saul. He said:

¹ I love you, LORD, my strength.

² The LORD is my rock, my fortress and my deliverer;
   my God is my rock, in whom I take refuge,
   my shield[b] and the horn[c] of my salvation, my stronghold.

³ I called to the LORD, who is worthy of praise,
   and I have been saved from my enemies.
⁴ The cords of death entangled me;
   the torrents of destruction overwhelmed me.
⁵ The cords of the grave coiled around me;
   the snares of death confronted me.

⁶ In my distress I called to the LORD;
   I cried to my God for help.
 From his temple he heard my voice;
   my cry came before him, into his ears.
⁷ The earth trembled and quaked,
   and the foundations of the mountains shook;
   they trembled because he was angry.
⁸ Smoke rose from his nostrils;
   consuming fire came from his mouth,
   burning coals blazed out of it.
⁹ He parted the heavens and came down;
   dark clouds were under his feet.
¹⁰ He mounted the cherubim and flew;
   he soared on the wings of the wind.
¹¹ He made darkness his covering, his canopy around him —
   the dark rain clouds of the sky.
¹² Out of the brightness of his presence clouds advanced,
   with hailstones and bolts of lightning.
¹³ The LORD thundered from heaven;
   the voice of the Most High resounded.[d]
¹⁴ He shot his arrows and scattered the enemy,
   with great bolts of lightning he routed them.
¹⁵ The valleys of the sea were exposed
   and the foundations of the earth laid bare
 at your rebuke, LORD,
   at the blast of breath from your nostrils.

---

[a] In Hebrew texts 18:1-50 is numbered 18:2-51.   [b] *2* Or *sovereign*   [c] *2 Horn* here symbolizes strength.
[d] *13* Some Hebrew manuscripts and Septuagint (see also 2 Samuel 22:14); most Hebrew manuscripts
resounded, / amid hailstones and bolts of lightning

[16] He reached down from on high and took hold of me;
    he drew me out of deep waters.
[17] He rescued me from my powerful enemy,
    from my foes, who were too strong for me.
[18] They confronted me in the day of my disaster,
    but the LORD was my support.
[19] He brought me out into a spacious place;
    he rescued me because he delighted in me.

[20] The LORD has dealt with me according to my righteousness;
    according to the cleanness of my hands he has rewarded me.
[21] For I have kept the ways of the LORD;
    I am not guilty of turning from my God.
[22] All his laws are before me;
    I have not turned away from his decrees.
[23] I have been blameless before him
    and have kept myself from sin.
[24] The LORD has rewarded me according to my righteousness,
    according to the cleanness of my hands in his sight.

[25] To the faithful you show yourself faithful,
    to the blameless you show yourself blameless,
[26] to the pure you show yourself pure,
    but to the devious you show yourself shrewd.
[27] You save the humble
    but bring low those whose eyes are haughty.
[28] You, LORD, keep my lamp burning;
    my God turns my darkness into light.
[29] With your help I can advance against a troop[a];
    with my God I can scale a wall.

[30] As for God, his way is perfect:
    The LORD's word is flawless;
    he shields all who take refuge in him.
[31] For who is God besides the LORD?
    And who is the Rock except our God?
[32] It is God who arms me with strength
    and keeps my way secure.
[33] He makes my feet like the feet of a deer;
    he causes me to stand on the heights.
[34] He trains my hands for battle;
    my arms can bend a bow of bronze.
[35] You make your saving help my shield,
    and your right hand sustains me;
    your help has made me great.
[36] You provide a broad path for my feet,
    so that my ankles do not give way.

[a] 29 Or can run through a barricade

37 I pursued my enemies and overtook them;
    I did not turn back till they were destroyed.
38 I crushed them so that they could not rise;
    they fell beneath my feet.
39 You armed me with strength for battle;
    you humbled my adversaries before me.
40 You made my enemies turn their backs in flight,
    and I destroyed my foes.
41 They cried for help, but there was no one to save them —
    to the LORD, but he did not answer.
42 I beat them as fine as windblown dust;
    I trampled them*a* like mud in the streets.
43 You have delivered me from the attacks of the people;
    you have made me the head of nations.
  People I did not know now serve me,
44   foreigners cower before me;
    as soon as they hear of me, they obey me.
45 They all lose heart;
    they come trembling from their strongholds.

46 The LORD lives! Praise be to my Rock!
    Exalted be God my Savior!
47 He is the God who avenges me,
    who subdues nations under me,
48   who saves me from my enemies.
  You exalted me above my foes;
    from a violent man you rescued me.
49 Therefore I will praise you, LORD, among the nations;
    I will sing the praises of your name.

50 He gives his king great victories;
    he shows unfailing love to his anointed,
    to David and to his descendants forever.

Psalm 19*b*

For the director of music. A psalm of David.

1 The heavens declare the glory of God;
    the skies proclaim the work of his hands.
2 Day after day they pour forth speech;
    night after night they reveal knowledge.
3 They have no speech, they use no words;
    no sound is heard from them.
4 Yet their voice*c* goes out into all the earth,
    their words to the ends of the world.
  In the heavens God has pitched a tent for the sun.

---

a 42 Many Hebrew manuscripts, Septuagint, Syriac and Targum (see also 2 Samuel 22:43); Masoretic Text *I poured them out*   *b* In Hebrew texts 19:1-14 is numbered 19:2-15.   *c* 4 Septuagint, Jerome and Syriac; Hebrew *measuring line*

In Control

Read Psalm 19:1–6. God placed the earth just far enough from the sun to give us light and warmth. He made the earth rotate so the warmth would be spread everywhere. He makes sure the sun rises and sets every day, just as it should. If you watch the sun do its work each day, it will show you that God is in control.

Go to a park with a parent or grandparent to watch the sunset. Let it be a reminder to you that God is in control from sunset to sunset, through all your life. In the space below, tell God about anything that is concerning you and thank him for being in control.

Psalm 19:1-6

⁵ It is like a bridegroom coming out of his chamber,
   like a champion rejoicing to run his course.
⁶ It rises at one end of the heavens
      and makes its circuit to the other;
      nothing is deprived of its warmth.

⁷ The law of the Lord is perfect,
      refreshing the soul.
   The statutes of the Lord are trustworthy,
      making wise the simple.
⁸ The precepts of the Lord are right,
      giving joy to the heart.
   The commands of the Lord are radiant,
      giving light to the eyes.
⁹ The fear of the Lord is pure,
      enduring forever.
   The decrees of the Lord are firm,
      and all of them are righteous.

¹⁰ They are more precious than gold,
      than much pure gold;
   they are sweeter than honey,
      than honey from the honeycomb.
¹¹ By them your servant is warned;
      in keeping them there is great reward.
¹² But who can discern their own errors?
      Forgive my hidden faults.
¹³ Keep your servant also from willful sins;
      may they not rule over me.
   Then I will be blameless,
      innocent of great transgression.

¹⁴ May these words of my mouth and this meditation of my heart
      be pleasing in your sight,
   Lord, my Rock and my Redeemer.

Psalm 20^a

For the director of music. A psalm of David.

¹ May the Lord answer you when you are in distress;
      may the name of the God of Jacob protect you.
² May he send you help from the sanctuary
      and grant you support from Zion.
³ May he remember all your sacrifices
      and accept your burnt offerings.^b
⁴ May he give you the desire of your heart
      and make all your plans succeed.
⁵ May we shout for joy over your victory
      and lift up our banners in the name of our God.

---

^a In Hebrew texts 20:1-9 is numbered 20:2-10.   ^b *3* The Hebrew has *Selah* (a word of uncertain meaning) here.

May the LORD grant all your requests.

6 Now this I know:
    The LORD gives victory to his anointed.
  He answers him from his heavenly sanctuary
    with the victorious power of his right hand.
7 Some trust in chariots and some in horses,
    but we trust in the name of the LORD our God.
8 They are brought to their knees and fall,
    but we rise up and stand firm.
9 LORD, give victory to the king!
    Answer us when we call!

Psalm 21[a]

For the director of music. A psalm of David.

1 The king rejoices in your strength, LORD.
    How great is his joy in the victories you give!

2 You have granted him his heart's desire
    and have not withheld the request of his lips.[b]
3 You came to greet him with rich blessings
    and placed a crown of pure gold on his head.
4 He asked you for life, and you gave it to him —
    length of days, for ever and ever.
5 Through the victories you gave, his glory is great;
    you have bestowed on him splendor and majesty.
6 Surely you have granted him unending blessings
    and made him glad with the joy of your presence.
7 For the king trusts in the LORD;
    through the unfailing love of the Most High
    he will not be shaken.

8 Your hand will lay hold on all your enemies;
    your right hand will seize your foes.
9 When you appear for battle,
    you will burn them up as in a blazing furnace.
  The LORD will swallow them up in his wrath,
    and his fire will consume them.
10 You will destroy their descendants from the earth,
    their posterity from mankind.
11 Though they plot evil against you
    and devise wicked schemes, they cannot succeed.
12 You will make them turn their backs
    when you aim at them with drawn bow.

13 Be exalted in your strength, LORD;
    we will sing and praise your might.

---

[a] In Hebrew texts 21:1-13 is numbered 21:2-14.   [b] 2 The Hebrew has *Selah* (a word of uncertain meaning) here.

Psalm 22[a]

*For the director of music. To the tune of "The
Doe of the Morning." A psalm of David.*

[1] My God, my God, why have you forsaken me?
    Why are you so far from saving me,
    so far from my cries of anguish?
[2] My God, I cry out by day, but you do not answer,
    by night, but I find no rest.[b]

[3] Yet you are enthroned as the Holy One;
    you are the one Israel praises.[c]
[4] In you our ancestors put their trust;
    they trusted and you delivered them.
[5] To you they cried out and were saved;
    in you they trusted and were not put to shame.

[6] But I am a worm and not a man,
    scorned by everyone, despised by the people.
[7] All who see me mock me;
    they hurl insults, shaking their heads.
[8] "He trusts in the LORD," they say,
    "let the LORD rescue him.
  Let him deliver him,
    since he delights in him."

[9] Yet you brought me out of the womb;
    you made me trust in you, even at my mother's breast.
[10] From birth I was cast on you;
    from my mother's womb you have been my God.

[11] Do not be far from me,
    for trouble is near
    and there is no one to help.

[12] Many bulls surround me;
    strong bulls of Bashan encircle me.
[13] Roaring lions that tear their prey
    open their mouths wide against me.
[14] I am poured out like water,
    and all my bones are out of joint.
  My heart has turned to wax;
    it has melted within me.
[15] My mouth[d] is dried up like a potsherd,
    and my tongue sticks to the roof of my mouth;
    you lay me in the dust of death.

---

[a] In Hebrew texts 22:1-31 is numbered 22:2-32.   [b] 2 Or *night, and am not silent*   [c] 3 Or *Yet you are holy, /
enthroned on the praises of Israel*   [d] 15 Probable reading of the original Hebrew text; Masoretic Text
strength

¹⁶ Dogs surround me,
    a pack of villains encircles me;
    they pierce[a] my hands and my feet.
¹⁷ All my bones are on display;
    people stare and gloat over me.
¹⁸ They divide my clothes among them
    and cast lots for my garment.

¹⁹ But you, LORD, do not be far from me.
    You are my strength; come quickly to help me.
²⁰ Deliver me from the sword,
    my precious life from the power of the dogs.
²¹ Rescue me from the mouth of the lions;
    save me from the horns of the wild oxen.

²² I will declare your name to my people;
    in the assembly I will praise you.
²³ You who fear the LORD, praise him!
    All you descendants of Jacob, honor him!
    Revere him, all you descendants of Israel!
²⁴ For he has not despised or scorned
    the suffering of the afflicted one;
  he has not hidden his face from him
    but has listened to his cry for help.

²⁵ From you comes the theme of my praise in the great assembly;
    before those who fear you[b] I will fulfill my vows.
²⁶ The poor will eat and be satisfied;
    those who seek the LORD will praise him —
    may your hearts live forever!

²⁷ All the ends of the earth
    will remember and turn to the LORD,
  and all the families of the nations
    will bow down before him,
²⁸ for dominion belongs to the LORD
    and he rules over the nations.

²⁹ All the rich of the earth will feast and worship;
    all who go down to the dust will kneel before him —
    those who cannot keep themselves alive.
³⁰ Posterity will serve him;
    future generations will be told about the Lord.
³¹ They will proclaim his righteousness,
    declaring to a people yet unborn:
    He has done it!

---

[a] 16 Dead Sea Scrolls and some manuscripts of the Masoretic Text, Septuagint and Syriac; most manuscripts of the Masoretic Text *me, / like a lion*   [b] 25 Hebrew *him*

Life in Bible Times

What God Is Like

Psalm 23 says that God is like a shepherd. A shepherd loves and cares for his sheep. He watches them closely, protects them from danger, and makes sure that they have enough to eat and drink. To say that God is our shepherd means that he watches over us and shows us what is best for us.

Psalm 23

A psalm of David.

¹The LORD is my shepherd, I lack nothing.
²   He makes me lie down in green pastures,
  he leads me beside quiet waters,
³   he refreshes my soul.
  He guides me along the right paths
      for his name's sake.
⁴Even though I walk
      through the darkest valley,ᵃ
  I will fear no evil,
      for you are with me;
  your rod and your staff,
      they comfort me.

⁵You prepare a table before me
      in the presence of my enemies.
  You anoint my head with oil;
      my cup overflows.
⁶Surely your goodness and love will follow me
      all the days of my life,
  and I will dwell in the house of the LORD
      forever.

Psalm 24

Of David. A psalm.

¹The earth is the LORD's, and everything in it,
      the world, and all who live in it;
²for he founded it on the seas
      and established it on the waters.

³Who may ascend the mountain of the LORD?
      Who may stand in his holy place?
⁴The one who has clean hands and a pure heart,
      who does not trust in an idol
      or swear by a false god.ᵇ

⁵They will receive blessing from the LORD
      and vindication from God their Savior.
⁶Such is the generation of those who seek him,
      who seek your face, God of Jacob.ᶜ,ᵈ

⁷Lift up your heads, you gates;
      be lifted up, you ancient doors,
      that the King of glory may come in.

ᵃ 4 Or *the valley of the shadow of death*   ᵇ 4 Or *swear falsely*   ᶜ 6 Two Hebrew manuscripts and Syriac
(see also Septuagint); most Hebrew manuscripts *face, Jacob*   ᵈ 6 The Hebrew has *Selah* (a word of
uncertain meaning) here and at the end of verse 10.

God Is My Shepherd

Read Psalm 23. God loves you, just as a shepherd loves his sheep. God wants to take care of you and protect you, just as a shepherd cares for and protects his sheep.

Ask someone to take a picture of you at a nearby park or wildlife area. Be sure the background includes green grass and a stream if possible. Put that picture somewhere in your room with a sticky note above it that says "The Lord Is My Shepherd." Let it be a reminder to you of God's care. Then, in the space below, write about a time God took care of you.

Live It!

Psalm 23:1–6

_____

_____

_____

_____

_____

_____

_____

_____

_____

_____

_____

_____

_____

_____

_____

_____

8 Who is this King of glory?
    The LORD strong and mighty,
    the LORD mighty in battle.
9 Lift up your heads, you gates;
    lift them up, you ancient doors,
    that the King of glory may come in.
10 Who is he, this King of glory?
    The LORD Almighty —
    he is the King of glory.

Psalm 25[a]

Of David.

1 In you, LORD my God,
    I put my trust.

2 I trust in you;
    do not let me be put to shame,
    nor let my enemies triumph over me.
3 No one who hopes in you
    will ever be put to shame,
  but shame will come on those
    who are treacherous without cause.

4 Show me your ways, LORD,
    teach me your paths.
5 Guide me in your truth and teach me,
    for you are God my Savior,
    and my hope is in you all day long.
6 Remember, LORD, your great mercy and love,
    for they are from of old.
7 Do not remember the sins of my youth
    and my rebellious ways;
  according to your love remember me,
    for you, LORD, are good.

8 Good and upright is the LORD;
    therefore he instructs sinners in his ways.
9 He guides the humble in what is right
    and teaches them his way.
10 All the ways of the LORD are loving and faithful
    toward those who keep the demands of his covenant.
11 For the sake of your name, LORD,
    forgive my iniquity, though it is great.

12 Who, then, are those who fear the LORD?
    He will instruct them in the ways they should choose.[b]
13 They will spend their days in prosperity,
    and their descendants will inherit the land.

---

[a] This psalm is an acrostic poem, the verses of which begin with the successive letters of the Hebrew alphabet.   [b] 12 Or *ways he chooses*

14 The LORD confides in those who fear him;
    he makes his covenant known to them.
15 My eyes are ever on the LORD,
    for only he will release my feet from the snare.

16 Turn to me and be gracious to me,
    for I am lonely and afflicted.
17 Relieve the troubles of my heart
    and free me from my anguish.
18 Look on my affliction and my distress
    and take away all my sins.
19 See how numerous are my enemies
    and how fiercely they hate me!

20 Guard my life and rescue me;
    do not let me be put to shame,
    for I take refuge in you.
21 May integrity and uprightness protect me,
    because my hope, LORD,[a] is in you.

22 Deliver Israel, O God,
    from all their troubles!

Psalm 26

Of David.

1 Vindicate me, LORD,
    for I have led a blameless life;
 I have trusted in the LORD
    and have not faltered.
2 Test me, LORD, and try me,
    examine my heart and my mind;
3 for I have always been mindful of your unfailing love
    and have lived in reliance on your faithfulness.

4 I do not sit with the deceitful,
    nor do I associate with hypocrites.
5 I abhor the assembly of evildoers
    and refuse to sit with the wicked.
6 I wash my hands in innocence,
    and go about your altar, LORD,
7 proclaiming aloud your praise
    and telling of all your wonderful deeds.

8 LORD, I love the house where you live,
    the place where your glory dwells.
9 Do not take away my soul along with sinners,
    my life with those who are bloodthirsty,
10 in whose hands are wicked schemes,
    whose right hands are full of bribes.

---

a 21 Septuagint; Hebrew does not have LORD.

11 I lead a blameless life;
   deliver me and be merciful to me.

12 My feet stand on level ground;
   in the great congregation I will praise the LORD.

Psalm 27

Of David.

1 The LORD is my light and my salvation —
   whom shall I fear?
 The LORD is the stronghold of my life —
   of whom shall I be afraid?

2 When the wicked advance against me
   to devour[a] me,
 it is my enemies and my foes
   who will stumble and fall.
3 Though an army besiege me,
   my heart will not fear;
 though war break out against me,
   even then I will be confident.

4 One thing I ask from the LORD,
   this only do I seek:
 that I may dwell in the house of the LORD
   all the days of my life,
 to gaze on the beauty of the LORD
   and to seek him in his temple.
5 For in the day of trouble
   he will keep me safe in his dwelling;
 he will hide me in the shelter of his sacred tent
   and set me high upon a rock.

6 Then my head will be exalted
   above the enemies who surround me;
 at his sacred tent I will sacrifice with shouts of joy;
   I will sing and make music to the LORD.

7 Hear my voice when I call, LORD;
   be merciful to me and answer me.
8 My heart says of you, "Seek his face!"
   Your face, LORD, I will seek.
9 Do not hide your face from me,
   do not turn your servant away in anger;
   you have been my helper.
 Do not reject me or forsake me,
   God my Savior.
10 Though my father and mother forsake me,
   the LORD will receive me.

a 2 Or *slander*

[11] Teach me your way, LORD;
　　lead me in a straight path
　　because of my oppressors.
[12] Do not turn me over to the desire of my foes,
　　for false witnesses rise up against me,
　　spouting malicious accusations.

[13] I remain confident of this:
　　I will see the goodness of the LORD
　　in the land of the living.
[14] Wait for the LORD;
　　be strong and take heart
　　and wait for the LORD.

Psalm 28

Of David.

[1] To you, LORD, I call;
　　you are my Rock,
　　do not turn a deaf ear to me.
　For if you remain silent,
　　I will be like those who go down to the pit.
[2] Hear my cry for mercy
　　as I call to you for help,
　as I lift up my hands
　　toward your Most Holy Place.

[3] Do not drag me away with the wicked,
　　with those who do evil,
　who speak cordially with their neighbors
　　but harbor malice in their hearts.
[4] Repay them for their deeds
　　and for their evil work;
　repay them for what their hands have done
　　and bring back on them what they deserve.

[5] Because they have no regard for the deeds of the LORD
　　and what his hands have done,
　he will tear them down
　　and never build them up again.

[6] Praise be to the LORD,
　　for he has heard my cry for mercy.
[7] The LORD is my strength and my shield;
　　my heart trusts in him, and he helps me.
　My heart leaps for joy,
　　and with my song I praise him.

[8] The LORD is the strength of his people,
　　a fortress of salvation for his anointed one.
[9] Save your people and bless your inheritance;
　　be their shepherd and carry them forever.

Psalm 29

A psalm of David.

[1]Ascribe to the LORD, you heavenly beings,
  ascribe to the LORD glory and strength.
[2]Ascribe to the LORD the glory due his name;
  worship the LORD in the splendor of his[a] holiness.

[3]The voice of the LORD is over the waters;
  the God of glory thunders,
  the LORD thunders over the mighty waters.
[4]The voice of the LORD is powerful;
  the voice of the LORD is majestic.
[5]The voice of the LORD breaks the cedars;
  the LORD breaks in pieces the cedars of Lebanon.
[6]He makes Lebanon leap like a calf,
  Sirion[b] like a young wild ox.
[7]The voice of the LORD strikes
  with flashes of lightning.
[8]The voice of the LORD shakes the desert;
  the LORD shakes the Desert of Kadesh.
[9]The voice of the LORD twists the oaks[c]
  and strips the forests bare.
 And in his temple all cry, "Glory!"

[10]The LORD sits enthroned over the flood;
  the LORD is enthroned as King forever.
[11]The LORD gives strength to his people;
  the LORD blesses his people with peace.

Psalm 30[d]

A psalm. A song. For the dedication of the temple.[e] Of David.

[1]I will exalt you, LORD,
  for you lifted me out of the depths
  and did not let my enemies gloat over me.
[2]LORD my God, I called to you for help,
  and you healed me.
[3]You, LORD, brought me up from the realm of the dead;
  you spared me from going down to the pit.

[4]Sing the praises of the LORD, you his faithful people;
  praise his holy name.
[5]For his anger lasts only a moment,
  but his favor lasts a lifetime;
 weeping may stay for the night,
  but rejoicing comes in the morning.

---

[a] 2 Or LORD *with the splendor of*   [b] 6 That is, Mount Hermon   [c] 9 Or LORD *makes the deer give birth*   [d] In Hebrew texts 30:1-12 is numbered 30:2-13.   [e] Title: Or *palace*

Good Things Ahead

Ask your mom or dad or grandparent about a time when one of them felt very sad. Why was he or she so sad? How long before the sadness went away? Ask too about times they felt very happy.

Then read Psalm 30:4–5. Sadness is like the night, when everything seems dark. But God says that joy will come in the morning. There are good things ahead for all of God's people. In the space below, answer the following question, "What recently brought you joy?"

Psalm 30:4–5

_____

_____

_____

_____

_____

_____

_____

_____

_____

_____

_____

_____

_____

_____

_____

6 When I felt secure, I said,
    "I will never be shaken."
7 LORD, when you favored me,
    you made my royal mountain[a] stand firm;
  but when you hid your face,
    I was dismayed.

8 To you, LORD, I called;
    to the Lord I cried for mercy:
9 "What is gained if I am silenced,
    if I go down to the pit?
  Will the dust praise you?
    Will it proclaim your faithfulness?
10 Hear, LORD, and be merciful to me;
    LORD, be my help."

11 You turned my wailing into dancing;
    you removed my sackcloth and clothed me with joy,
12 that my heart may sing your praises and not be silent.
    LORD my God, I will praise you forever.

Psalm 31[b]

For the director of music. A psalm of David.

1 In you, LORD, I have taken refuge;
    let me never be put to shame;
    deliver me in your righteousness.
2 Turn your ear to me,
    come quickly to my rescue;
  be my rock of refuge,
    a strong fortress to save me.
3 Since you are my rock and my fortress,
    for the sake of your name lead and guide me.
4 Keep me free from the trap that is set for me,
    for you are my refuge.
5 Into your hands I commit my spirit;
    deliver me, LORD, my faithful God.

6 I hate those who cling to worthless idols;
    as for me, I trust in the LORD.
7 I will be glad and rejoice in your love,
    for you saw my affliction
    and knew the anguish of my soul.
8 You have not given me into the hands of the enemy
    but have set my feet in a spacious place.

9 Be merciful to me, LORD, for I am in distress;
    my eyes grow weak with sorrow,
    my soul and body with grief.

---

a 7 That is, Mount Zion   *b* In Hebrew texts 31:1-24 is numbered 31:2-25.

¹⁰ My life is consumed by anguish
    and my years by groaning;
  my strength fails because of my affliction,ᵃ
    and my bones grow weak.
¹¹ Because of all my enemies,
    I am the utter contempt of my neighbors
  and an object of dread to my closest friends —
    those who see me on the street flee from me.
¹² I am forgotten as though I were dead;
    I have become like broken pottery.
¹³ For I hear many whispering,
    "Terror on every side!"
  They conspire against me
    and plot to take my life.

¹⁴ But I trust in you, Lord;
    I say, "You are my God."
¹⁵ My times are in your hands;
    deliver me from the hands of my enemies,
    from those who pursue me.
¹⁶ Let your face shine on your servant;
    save me in your unfailing love.
¹⁷ Let me not be put to shame, Lord,
    for I have cried out to you;
  but let the wicked be put to shame
    and be silent in the realm of the dead.
¹⁸ Let their lying lips be silenced,
    for with pride and contempt
    they speak arrogantly against the righteous.

¹⁹ How abundant are the good things
    that you have stored up for those who fear you,
  that you bestow in the sight of all,
    on those who take refuge in you.
²⁰ In the shelter of your presence you hide them
    from all human intrigues;
  you keep them safe in your dwelling
    from accusing tongues.

²¹ Praise be to the Lord,
    for he showed me the wonders of his love
    when I was in a city under siege.
²² In my alarm I said,
    "I am cut off from your sight!"
  Yet you heard my cry for mercy
    when I called to you for help.

ᵃ 10 Or *guilt*

23 Love the LORD, all his faithful people!
　　The LORD preserves those who are true to him,
　　but the proud he pays back in full.
24 Be strong and take heart,
　　all you who hope in the LORD.

Psalm 32

Of David. A maskil.[a]

1 Blessed is the one
　　whose transgressions are forgiven,
　　whose sins are covered.
2 Blessed is the one
　　whose sin the LORD does not count against them
　　and in whose spirit is no deceit.

3 When I kept silent,
　　my bones wasted away
　　through my groaning all day long.
4 For day and night
　　your hand was heavy on me;
　my strength was sapped
　　as in the heat of summer.[b]

5 Then I acknowledged my sin to you
　　and did not cover up my iniquity.
　I said, "I will confess
　　my transgressions to the LORD."
　And you forgave
　　the guilt of my sin.

6 Therefore let all the faithful pray to you
　　while you may be found;
　surely the rising of the mighty waters
　　will not reach them.
7 You are my hiding place;
　　you will protect me from trouble
　　and surround me with songs of deliverance.

8 I will instruct you and teach you in the way you should go;
　　I will counsel you with my loving eye on you.
9 Do not be like the horse or the mule,
　　which have no understanding
　but must be controlled by bit and bridle
　　or they will not come to you.
10 Many are the woes of the wicked,
　　but the LORD's unfailing love
　　surrounds the one who trusts in him.

11 Rejoice in the LORD and be glad, you righteous;
　　sing, all you who are upright in heart!

---

[a] Title: Probably a literary or musical term　　[b] 4 The Hebrew has *Selah* (a word of uncertain meaning) here
and at the end of verses 5 and 7.

Admit Sins and Feel Better

Even Bible heroes like David sinned. This psalm tells how David felt when he did wrong.

Read Psalm 32:3–4. Can you think of three times when you did something wrong and felt very bad, as David did?

Psalm 32:5 tells what David did to feel better. He admitted (confessed) his sin to God. Then God forgave David, and he felt better.

Ask your mom for some nail polish, and paint one side of a quarter red. The red represents sin and the unhappiness we feel when we've done something

Psalm 32:3–5

wrong. The shiny other side represents admitting sins to God and being forgiven. Flip the coin. Any time it comes up red you can turn it over, to remind you that whenever you sin you can confess your sin to God and be forgiven.

Psalm 33

¹ Sing joyfully to the LORD, you righteous;
  it is fitting for the upright to praise him.
² Praise the LORD with the harp;
  make music to him on the ten-stringed lyre.
³ Sing to him a new song;
  play skillfully, and shout for joy.

⁴ For the word of the LORD is right and true;
  he is faithful in all he does.
⁵ The LORD loves righteousness and justice;
  the earth is full of his unfailing love.

⁶ By the word of the LORD the heavens were made,
  their starry host by the breath of his mouth.
⁷ He gathers the waters of the sea into jars[a];
  he puts the deep into storehouses.
⁸ Let all the earth fear the LORD;
  let all the people of the world revere him.
⁹ For he spoke, and it came to be;
  he commanded, and it stood firm.

¹⁰ The LORD foils the plans of the nations;
  he thwarts the purposes of the peoples.
¹¹ But the plans of the LORD stand firm forever,
  the purposes of his heart through all generations.

¹² Blessed is the nation whose God is the LORD,
  the people he chose for his inheritance.
¹³ From heaven the LORD looks down
  and sees all mankind;
¹⁴ from his dwelling place he watches
  all who live on earth —
¹⁵ he who forms the hearts of all,
  who considers everything they do.

¹⁶ No king is saved by the size of his army;
  no warrior escapes by his great strength.
¹⁷ A horse is a vain hope for deliverance;
  despite all its great strength it cannot save.
¹⁸ But the eyes of the LORD are on those who fear him,
  on those whose hope is in his unfailing love,
¹⁹ to deliver them from death
  and keep them alive in famine.

²⁰ We wait in hope for the LORD;
  he is our help and our shield.
²¹ In him our hearts rejoice,
  for we trust in his holy name.
²² May your unfailing love be with us, LORD,
  even as we put our hope in you.

---

a 7 Or sea as into a heap

Psalm 34[a,b]

Of David. When he pretended to be insane before
Abimelek, who drove him away, and he left.

¹I will extol the LORD at all times;
    his praise will always be on my lips.
²I will glory in the LORD;
    let the afflicted hear and rejoice.
³Glorify the LORD with me;
    let us exalt his name together.

⁴I sought the LORD, and he answered me;
    he delivered me from all my fears.
⁵Those who look to him are radiant;
    their faces are never covered with shame.
⁶This poor man called, and the LORD heard him;
    he saved him out of all his troubles.
⁷The angel of the LORD encamps around those who fear him,
    and he delivers them.

⁸Taste and see that the LORD is good;
    blessed is the one who takes refuge in him.
⁹Fear the LORD, you his holy people,
    for those who fear him lack nothing.
¹⁰The lions may grow weak and hungry,
    but those who seek the LORD lack no good thing.
¹¹Come, my children, listen to me;
    I will teach you the fear of the LORD.
¹²Whoever of you loves life
    and desires to see many good days,
¹³keep your tongue from evil
    and your lips from telling lies.
¹⁴Turn from evil and do good;
    seek peace and pursue it.

¹⁵The eyes of the LORD are on the righteous,
    and his ears are attentive to their cry;
¹⁶but the face of the LORD is against those who do evil,
    to blot out their name from the earth.

¹⁷The righteous cry out, and the LORD hears them;
    he delivers them from all their troubles.
¹⁸The LORD is close to the brokenhearted
    and saves those who are crushed in spirit.

¹⁹The righteous person may have many troubles,
    but the LORD delivers him from them all;
²⁰he protects all his bones,
    not one of them will be broken.

---

[a] This psalm is an acrostic poem, the verses of which begin with the successive letters of the Hebrew alphabet.   [b] In Hebrew texts 34:1-22 is numbered 34:2-23.

²¹ Evil will slay the wicked;
    the foes of the righteous will be condemned.
²² The LORD will rescue his servants;
    no one who takes refuge in him will be condemned.

Psalm 35

Of David.

¹ Contend, LORD, with those who contend with me;
    fight against those who fight against me.
² Take up shield and armor;
    arise and come to my aid.
³ Brandish spear and javelin*
    against those who pursue me.
 Say to me,
    "I am your salvation."

⁴ May those who seek my life
    be disgraced and put to shame;
 may those who plot my ruin
    be turned back in dismay.
⁵ May they be like chaff before the wind,
    with the angel of the LORD driving them away;
⁶ may their path be dark and slippery,
    with the angel of the LORD pursuing them.

⁷ Since they hid their net for me without cause
    and without cause dug a pit for me,
⁸ may ruin overtake them by surprise —
    may the net they hid entangle them,
    may they fall into the pit, to their ruin.
⁹ Then my soul will rejoice in the LORD
    and delight in his salvation.
¹⁰ My whole being will exclaim,
    "Who is like you, LORD?
 You rescue the poor from those too strong for them,
    the poor and needy from those who rob them."

¹¹ Ruthless witnesses come forward;
    they question me on things I know nothing about.
¹² They repay me evil for good
    and leave me like one bereaved.
¹³ Yet when they were ill, I put on sackcloth
    and humbled myself with fasting.
 When my prayers returned to me unanswered,
¹⁴   I went about mourning
    as though for my friend or brother.
 I bowed my head in grief
    as though weeping for my mother.

---

a 3 Or and block the way

¹⁵ But when I stumbled, they gathered in glee;
    assailants gathered against me without my knowledge.
    They slandered me without ceasing.
¹⁶ Like the ungodly they maliciously mocked;ᵃ
    they gnashed their teeth at me.

¹⁷ How long, Lord, will you look on?
    Rescue me from their ravages,
    my precious life from these lions.
¹⁸ I will give you thanks in the great assembly;
    among the throngs I will praise you.
¹⁹ Do not let those gloat over me
    who are my enemies without cause;
  do not let those who hate me without reason
    maliciously wink the eye.
²⁰ They do not speak peaceably,
    but devise false accusations
    against those who live quietly in the land.
²¹ They sneer at me and say, "Aha! Aha!
    With our own eyes we have seen it."

²² Lᴏʀᴅ, you have seen this; do not be silent.
    Do not be far from me, Lord.
²³ Awake, and rise to my defense!
    Contend for me, my God and Lord.
²⁴ Vindicate me in your righteousness, Lᴏʀᴅ my God;
    do not let them gloat over me.
²⁵ Do not let them think, "Aha, just what we wanted!"
    or say, "We have swallowed him up."

²⁶ May all who gloat over my distress
    be put to shame and confusion;
  may all who exalt themselves over me
    be clothed with shame and disgrace.
²⁷ May those who delight in my vindication
    shout for joy and gladness;
  may they always say, "The Lᴏʀᴅ be exalted,
    who delights in the well-being of his servant."

²⁸ My tongue will proclaim your righteousness,
    your praises all day long.

Psalm 36ᵇ

For the director of music. Of David the servant of the Lᴏʀᴅ.

¹ I have a message from God in my heart
    concerning the sinfulness of the wicked:ᶜ
  There is no fear of God
    before their eyes.

ᵃ 16 Septuagint; Hebrew may mean *Like an ungodly circle of mockers,*   ᵇ In Hebrew texts 36:1-12 is numbered 36:2-13.   ᶜ 1 Or *A message from God: The transgression of the wicked / resides in their hearts.*

²In their own eyes they flatter themselves
    too much to detect or hate their sin.
³The words of their mouths are wicked and deceitful;
    they fail to act wisely or do good.
⁴Even on their beds they plot evil;
    they commit themselves to a sinful course
    and do not reject what is wrong.

⁵Your love, LORD, reaches to the heavens,
    your faithfulness to the skies.
⁶Your righteousness is like the highest mountains,
    your justice like the great deep.
    You, LORD, preserve both people and animals.
⁷How priceless is your unfailing love, O God!
    People take refuge in the shadow of your wings.
⁸They feast on the abundance of your house;
    you give them drink from your river of delights.
⁹For with you is the fountain of life;
    in your light we see light.

¹⁰Continue your love to those who know you,
    your righteousness to the upright in heart.
¹¹May the foot of the proud not come against me,
    nor the hand of the wicked drive me away.
¹²See how the evildoers lie fallen —
    thrown down, not able to rise!

Psalm 37[a]

Of David.

¹Do not fret because of those who are evil
    or be envious of those who do wrong;
²for like the grass they will soon wither,
    like green plants they will soon die away.

³Trust in the LORD and do good;
    dwell in the land and enjoy safe pasture.
⁴Take delight in the LORD,
    and he will give you the desires of your heart.

⁵Commit your way to the LORD;
    trust in him and he will do this:
⁶He will make your righteous reward shine like the dawn,
    your vindication like the noonday sun.

⁷Be still before the LORD
    and wait patiently for him;
 do not fret when people succeed in their ways,
    when they carry out their wicked schemes.

[a] This psalm is an acrostic poem, the stanzas of which begin with the successive letters of the Hebrew alphabet.

⁸ Refrain from anger and turn from wrath;
     do not fret — it leads only to evil.
⁹ For those who are evil will be destroyed,
     but those who hope in the LORD will inherit the land.

¹⁰ A little while, and the wicked will be no more;
     though you look for them, they will not be found.
¹¹ But the meek will inherit the land
     and enjoy peace and prosperity.

¹² The wicked plot against the righteous
     and gnash their teeth at them;
¹³ but the Lord laughs at the wicked,
     for he knows their day is coming.

¹⁴ The wicked draw the sword
     and bend the bow
   to bring down the poor and needy,
     to slay those whose ways are upright.
¹⁵ But their swords will pierce their own hearts,
     and their bows will be broken.

¹⁶ Better the little that the righteous have
     than the wealth of many wicked;
¹⁷ for the power of the wicked will be broken,
     but the LORD upholds the righteous.

¹⁸ The blameless spend their days under the LORD's care,
     and their inheritance will endure forever.
¹⁹ In times of disaster they will not wither;
     in days of famine they will enjoy plenty.

²⁰ But the wicked will perish:
     Though the LORD's enemies are like the flowers of the field,
     they will be consumed, they will go up in smoke.

²¹ The wicked borrow and do not repay,
     but the righteous give generously;
²² those the LORD blesses will inherit the land,
     but those he curses will be destroyed.

²³ The LORD makes firm the steps
     of the one who delights in him;
²⁴ though he may stumble, he will not fall,
     for the LORD upholds him with his hand.

²⁵ I was young and now I am old,
     yet I have never seen the righteous forsaken
     or their children begging bread.
²⁶ They are always generous and lend freely;
     their children will be a blessing.ᵃ

ᵃ 26 Or freely; / the names of their children will be used in blessings (see Gen. 48:20); or freely; / others will see that their children are blessed

²⁷ Turn from evil and do good;
　　then you will dwell in the land forever.
²⁸ For the LORD loves the just
　　and will not forsake his faithful ones.

　Wrongdoers will be completely destroyed[a];
　　the offspring of the wicked will perish.
²⁹ The righteous will inherit the land
　　and dwell in it forever.

³⁰ The mouths of the righteous utter wisdom,
　　and their tongues speak what is just.
³¹ The law of their God is in their hearts;
　　their feet do not slip.

³² The wicked lie in wait for the righteous,
　　intent on putting them to death;
³³ but the LORD will not leave them in the power of the wicked
　　or let them be condemned when brought to trial.

³⁴ Hope in the LORD
　　and keep his way.
　He will exalt you to inherit the land;
　　when the wicked are destroyed, you will see it.

³⁵ I have seen a wicked and ruthless man
　　flourishing like a luxuriant native tree,
³⁶ but he soon passed away and was no more;
　　though I looked for him, he could not be found.

³⁷ Consider the blameless, observe the upright;
　　a future awaits those who seek peace.[b]
³⁸ But all sinners will be destroyed;
　　there will be no future[c] for the wicked.

³⁹ The salvation of the righteous comes from the LORD;
　　he is their stronghold in time of trouble.
⁴⁰ The LORD helps them and delivers them;
　　he delivers them from the wicked and saves them,
　　because they take refuge in him.

Psalm 38[d]

A psalm of David. A petition.

¹ LORD, do not rebuke me in your anger
　　or discipline me in your wrath.
² Your arrows have pierced me,
　　and your hand has come down on me.
³ Because of your wrath there is no health in my body;
　　there is no soundness in my bones because of my sin.

---

[a] 28 See Septuagint; Hebrew *They will be protected forever*　　[b] 37 Or *upright; / those who seek peace will have posterity*　　[c] 38 Or *posterity*　　[d] In Hebrew texts 38:1-22 is numbered 38:2-23.

Life in Bible Times

What God Is Like

Psalm 38 pictures God as an archer. His arrows wound a person who does wrong. But God hurts us only to help us. When we feel bad about doing wrong, we confess our sins. Then God will forgive and heal us.

⁴My guilt has overwhelmed me
    like a burden too heavy to bear.

⁵My wounds fester and are loathsome
    because of my sinful folly.
⁶I am bowed down and brought very low;
    all day long I go about mourning.
⁷My back is filled with searing pain;
    there is no health in my body.
⁸I am feeble and utterly crushed;
    I groan in anguish of heart.

⁹All my longings lie open before you, Lord;
    my sighing is not hidden from you.
¹⁰My heart pounds, my strength fails me;
    even the light has gone from my eyes.
¹¹My friends and companions avoid me because of my wounds;
    my neighbors stay far away.
¹²Those who want to kill me set their traps,
    those who would harm me talk of my ruin;
    all day long they scheme and lie.

¹³I am like the deaf, who cannot hear,
    like the mute, who cannot speak;
¹⁴I have become like one who does not hear,
    whose mouth can offer no reply.
¹⁵LORD, I wait for you;
    you will answer, Lord my God.
¹⁶For I said, "Do not let them gloat
    or exalt themselves over me when my feet slip."

¹⁷For I am about to fall,
    and my pain is ever with me.
¹⁸I confess my iniquity;
    I am troubled by my sin.
¹⁹Many have become my enemies without cause[a];
    those who hate me without reason are numerous.
²⁰Those who repay my good with evil
    lodge accusations against me,
    though I seek only to do what is good.

²¹LORD, do not forsake me;
    do not be far from me, my God.
²²Come quickly to help me,
    my Lord and my Savior.

---

[a] 19 One Dead Sea Scrolls manuscript; Masoretic Text *my vigorous enemies*

Psalm 39[a]

For the director of music. For Jeduthun. A psalm of David.

[1] I said, "I will watch my ways
    and keep my tongue from sin;
 I will put a muzzle on my mouth
    while in the presence of the wicked."
[2] So I remained utterly silent,
    not even saying anything good.
 But my anguish increased;
[3]   my heart grew hot within me.
 While I meditated, the fire burned;
    then I spoke with my tongue:

[4] "Show me, LORD, my life's end
    and the number of my days;
    let me know how fleeting my life is.
[5] You have made my days a mere handbreadth;
    the span of my years is as nothing before you.
 Everyone is but a breath,
    even those who seem secure.[b]

[6] "Surely everyone goes around like a mere phantom;
    in vain they rush about, heaping up wealth
    without knowing whose it will finally be.

[7] "But now, Lord, what do I look for?
    My hope is in you.
[8] Save me from all my transgressions;
    do not make me the scorn of fools.
[9] I was silent; I would not open my mouth,
    for you are the one who has done this.
[10] Remove your scourge from me;
    I am overcome by the blow of your hand.
[11] When you rebuke and discipline anyone for their sin,
    you consume their wealth like a moth —
    surely everyone is but a breath.

[12] "Hear my prayer, LORD,
    listen to my cry for help;
    do not be deaf to my weeping.
 I dwell with you as a foreigner,
    a stranger, as all my ancestors were.
[13] Look away from me, that I may enjoy life again
    before I depart and am no more."

---

[a] In Hebrew texts 39:1-13 is numbered 39:2-14.   [b] 5 The Hebrew has *Selah* (a word of uncertain meaning) here and at the end of verse 11.

Psalm 40[a]

For the director of music. Of David. A psalm.

1 I waited patiently for the LORD;
  he turned to me and heard my cry.
2 He lifted me out of the slimy pit,
  out of the mud and mire;
 he set my feet on a rock
  and gave me a firm place to stand.
3 He put a new song in my mouth,
  a hymn of praise to our God.
 Many will see and fear the LORD
  and put their trust in him.

4 Blessed is the one
  who trusts in the LORD,
 who does not look to the proud,
  to those who turn aside to false gods.[b]
5 Many, LORD my God,
  are the wonders you have done,
  the things you planned for us.
 None can compare with you;
  were I to speak and tell of your deeds,
  they would be too many to declare.

6 Sacrifice and offering you did not desire —
  but my ears you have opened[c] —
  burnt offerings and sin offerings[d] you did not require.
7 Then I said, "Here I am, I have come —
  it is written about me in the scroll.[e]
8 I desire to do your will, my God;
  your law is within my heart."

9 I proclaim your saving acts in the great assembly;
  I do not seal my lips, LORD,
  as you know.
10 I do not hide your righteousness in my heart;
  I speak of your faithfulness and your saving help.
 I do not conceal your love and your faithfulness
  from the great assembly.

11 Do not withhold your mercy from me, LORD;
  may your love and faithfulness always protect me.
12 For troubles without number surround me;
  my sins have overtaken me, and I cannot see.
 They are more than the hairs of my head,
  and my heart fails within me.

---

[a] In Hebrew texts 40:1-17 is numbered 40:2-18.   [b] 4 Or *to lies*   [c] 6 Hebrew; some Septuagint manuscripts *but a body you have prepared for me*   [d] 6 Or *purification offerings*   [e] 7 Or *come / with the scroll written for me*

¹³ Be pleased to save me, LORD;
     come quickly, LORD, to help me.

¹⁴ May all who want to take my life
     be put to shame and confusion;
   may all who desire my ruin
     be turned back in disgrace.
¹⁵ May those who say to me, "Aha! Aha!"
     be appalled at their own shame.
¹⁶ But may all who seek you
     rejoice and be glad in you;
   may those who long for your saving help always say,
     "The LORD is great!"

¹⁷ But as for me, I am poor and needy;
     may the Lord think of me.
   You are my help and my deliverer;
     you are my God, do not delay.

Psalm 41[a]

For the director of music. A psalm of David.

¹ Blessed are those who have regard for the weak;
     the LORD delivers them in times of trouble.
² The LORD protects and preserves them —
     they are counted among the blessed in the land —
   he does not give them over to the desire of their foes.
³ The LORD sustains them on their sickbed
     and restores them from their bed of illness.

⁴ I said, "Have mercy on me, LORD;
     heal me, for I have sinned against you."
⁵ My enemies say of me in malice,
     "When will he die and his name perish?"
⁶ When one of them comes to see me,
     he speaks falsely, while his heart gathers slander;
     then he goes out and spreads it around.

⁷ All my enemies whisper together against me;
     they imagine the worst for me, saying,
⁸ "A vile disease has afflicted him;
     he will never get up from the place where he lies."
⁹ Even my close friend,
     someone I trusted,
   one who shared my bread,
     has turned[b] against me.

¹⁰ But may you have mercy on me, LORD;
     raise me up, that I may repay them.

---

[a] In Hebrew texts 41:1-13 is numbered 41:2-14.   [b] 9 Hebrew *has lifted up his heel*

¹¹I know that you are pleased with me,
　　for my enemy does not triumph over me.
¹²Because of my integrity you uphold me
　　and set me in your presence forever.

¹³Praise be to the LORD, the God of Israel,
　　from everlasting to everlasting.
　　　　　　　　　　Amen and Amen.

BOOK II

Psalms 42 – 72

Psalm 42^{a,b}

For the director of music. A maskil^c of the Sons of Korah.

¹As the deer pants for streams of water,
　　so my soul pants for you, my God.
²My soul thirsts for God, for the living God.
　　When can I go and meet with God?
³My tears have been my food
　　day and night,
　while people say to me all day long,
　　"Where is your God?"
⁴These things I remember
　　as I pour out my soul:
　how I used to go to the house of God
　　under the protection of the Mighty One^d
　with shouts of joy and praise
　　among the festive throng.

⁵Why, my soul, are you downcast?
　　Why so disturbed within me?
　Put your hope in God,
　　for I will yet praise him,
　　my Savior and my God.

⁶My soul is downcast within me;
　　therefore I will remember you
　from the land of the Jordan,
　　the heights of Hermon — from Mount Mizar.
⁷Deep calls to deep
　　in the roar of your waterfalls;
　all your waves and breakers
　　have swept over me.

---

^a In many Hebrew manuscripts Psalms 42 and 43 constitute one psalm.　　^b In Hebrew texts 42:1-11 is numbered 42:2-12.　　^c Title: Probably a literary or musical term　　^d 4　See Septuagint and Syriac; the meaning of the Hebrew for this line is uncertain.

8 By day the LORD directs his love,
  at night his song is with me —
  a prayer to the God of my life.

9 I say to God my Rock,
  "Why have you forgotten me?
  Why must I go about mourning,
  oppressed by the enemy?"
10 My bones suffer mortal agony
  as my foes taunt me,
  saying to me all day long,
  "Where is your God?"

11 Why, my soul, are you downcast?
  Why so disturbed within me?
  Put your hope in God,
  for I will yet praise him,
  my Savior and my God.

Psalm 43[a]

1 Vindicate me, my God,
  and plead my cause
  against an unfaithful nation.
  Rescue me from those who are
  deceitful and wicked.
2 You are God my stronghold.
  Why have you rejected me?
  Why must I go about mourning,
  oppressed by the enemy?
3 Send me your light and your faithful care,
  let them lead me;
  let them bring me to your holy mountain,
  to the place where you dwell.
4 Then I will go to the altar of God,
  to God, my joy and my delight.
  I will praise you with the lyre,
  O God, my God.

5 Why, my soul, are you downcast?
  Why so disturbed within me?
  Put your hope in God,
  for I will yet praise him,
  my Savior and my God.

[a] In many Hebrew manuscripts Psalms 42 and 43 constitute one psalm.

Psalm 44[a]

For the director of music. Of the Sons of Korah. A maskil.[b]

[1]We have heard it with our ears, O God;
  our ancestors have told us
 what you did in their days,
  in days long ago.
[2]With your hand you drove out the nations
  and planted our ancestors;
 you crushed the peoples
  and made our ancestors flourish.
[3]It was not by their sword that they won the land,
  nor did their arm bring them victory;
 it was your right hand, your arm,
  and the light of your face, for you loved them.

[4]You are my King and my God,
  who decrees[c] victories for Jacob.
[5]Through you we push back our enemies;
  through your name we trample our foes.
[6]I put no trust in my bow,
  my sword does not bring me victory;
[7]but you give us victory over our enemies,
  you put our adversaries to shame.
[8]In God we make our boast all day long,
  and we will praise your name forever.[d]

[9]But now you have rejected and humbled us;
  you no longer go out with our armies.
[10]You made us retreat before the enemy,
  and our adversaries have plundered us.
[11]You gave us up to be devoured like sheep
  and have scattered us among the nations.
[12]You sold your people for a pittance,
  gaining nothing from their sale.

[13]You have made us a reproach to our neighbors,
  the scorn and derision of those around us.
[14]You have made us a byword among the nations;
  the peoples shake their heads at us.
[15]I live in disgrace all day long,
  and my face is covered with shame
[16]at the taunts of those who reproach and revile me,
  because of the enemy, who is bent on revenge.

[17]All this came upon us,
  though we had not forgotten you;
  we had not been false to your covenant.

---

[a] In Hebrew texts 44:1-26 is numbered 44:2-27.   [b] Title: Probably a literary or musical term   [c] 4 Septuagint, Aquila and Syriac; Hebrew *King, O God; / command*   [d] 8 The Hebrew has *Selah* (a word of uncertain meaning) here.

¹⁸ Our hearts had not turned back;
    our feet had not strayed from your path.
¹⁹ But you crushed us and made us a haunt for jackals;
    you covered us over with deep darkness.

²⁰ If we had forgotten the name of our God
    or spread out our hands to a foreign god,
²¹ would not God have discovered it,
    since he knows the secrets of the heart?
²² Yet for your sake we face death all day long;
    we are considered as sheep to be slaughtered.

²³ Awake, Lord! Why do you sleep?
    Rouse yourself! Do not reject us forever.
²⁴ Why do you hide your face
    and forget our misery and oppression?

²⁵ We are brought down to the dust;
    our bodies cling to the ground.
²⁶ Rise up and help us;
    rescue us because of your unfailing love.

Psalm 45[a]

*For the director of music. To the tune of "Lilies." Of the
Sons of Korah. A maskil.[b] A wedding song.*

¹ My heart is stirred by a noble theme
    as I recite my verses for the king;
    my tongue is the pen of a skillful writer.

² You are the most excellent of men
    and your lips have been anointed with grace,
    since God has blessed you forever.

³ Gird your sword on your side, you mighty one;
    clothe yourself with splendor and majesty.
⁴ In your majesty ride forth victoriously
    in the cause of truth, humility and justice;
    let your right hand achieve awesome deeds.
⁵ Let your sharp arrows pierce the hearts of the king's enemies;
    let the nations fall beneath your feet.
⁶ Your throne, O God,[c] will last for ever and ever;
    a scepter of justice will be the scepter of your kingdom.
⁷ You love righteousness and hate wickedness;
    therefore God, your God, has set you above your companions
    by anointing you with the oil of joy.
⁸ All your robes are fragrant with myrrh and aloes and cassia;
    from palaces adorned with ivory
    the music of the strings makes you glad.

---

[a] In Hebrew texts 45:1-17 is numbered 45:2-18.   [b] Title: Probably a literary or musical term   [c] 6 Here the king is addressed as God's representative.

⁹Daughters of kings are among your honored women;
    at your right hand is the royal bride in gold of Ophir.

¹⁰Listen, daughter, and pay careful attention:
    Forget your people and your father's house.
¹¹Let the king be enthralled by your beauty;
    honor him, for he is your lord.
¹²The city of Tyre will come with a gift,ᵃ
    people of wealth will seek your favor.
¹³All glorious is the princess within her chamber;
    her gown is interwoven with gold.
¹⁴In embroidered garments she is led to the king;
    her virgin companions follow her—
    those brought to be with her.
¹⁵Led in with joy and gladness,
    they enter the palace of the king.

¹⁶Your sons will take the place of your fathers;
    you will make them princes throughout the land.

¹⁷I will perpetuate your memory through all generations;
    therefore the nations will praise you for ever and ever.

Psalm 46ᵇ

For the director of music. Of the Sons of Korah.
According to alamoth.ᶜ *A song.*

¹God is our refuge and strength,
    an ever-present help in trouble.
²Therefore we will not fear, though the earth give way
    and the mountains fall into the heart of the sea,
³though its waters roar and foam
    and the mountains quake with their surging.ᵈ

⁴There is a river whose streams make glad the city of God,
    the holy place where the Most High dwells.
⁵God is within her, she will not fall;
    God will help her at break of day.
⁶Nations are in uproar, kingdoms fall;
    he lifts his voice, the earth melts.

⁷The Lᴏʀᴅ Almighty is with us;
    the God of Jacob is our fortress.

⁸Come and see what the Lᴏʀᴅ has done,
    the desolations he has brought on the earth.
⁹He makes wars cease
    to the ends of the earth.

ᵃ 12 Or *A Tyrian robe is among the gifts*   ᵇ In Hebrew texts 46:1-11 is numbered 46:2-12.   ᶜ Title: Probably a musical term   ᵈ 3 The Hebrew has *Selah* (a word of uncertain meaning) here and at the end of verses 7 and 11.

He breaks the bow and shatters the spear;
    he burns the shields[a] with fire.
[10] He says, "Be still, and know that I am God;
    I will be exalted among the nations,
    I will be exalted in the earth."

[11] The LORD Almighty is with us;
    the God of Jacob is our fortress.

Psalm 47[b]

For the director of music. Of the Sons of Korah. A psalm.

[1] Clap your hands, all you nations;
    shout to God with cries of joy.

[2] For the LORD Most High is awesome,
    the great King over all the earth.
[3] He subdued nations under us,
    peoples under our feet.
[4] He chose our inheritance for us,
    the pride of Jacob, whom he loved.[c]

[5] God has ascended amid shouts of joy,
    the LORD amid the sounding of trumpets.
[6] Sing praises to God, sing praises;
    sing praises to our King, sing praises.
[7] For God is the King of all the earth;
    sing to him a psalm of praise.

[8] God reigns over the nations;
    God is seated on his holy throne.
[9] The nobles of the nations assemble
    as the people of the God of Abraham,
for the kings[d] of the earth belong to God;
    he is greatly exalted.

Psalm 48[e]

A song. A psalm of the Sons of Korah.

[1] Great is the LORD, and most worthy of praise,
    in the city of our God, his holy mountain.

[2] Beautiful in its loftiness,
    the joy of the whole earth,
like the heights of Zaphon[f] is Mount Zion,
    the city of the Great King.
[3] God is in her citadels;
    he has shown himself to be her fortress.

[a] 9 Or *chariots*   [b] In Hebrew texts 47:1-9 is numbered 47:2-10.   [c] 4 The Hebrew has *Selah* (a word of uncertain meaning) here.   [d] 9 Or *shields*   [e] In Hebrew texts 48:1-14 is numbered 48:2-15.   [f] 2 *Zaphon* was the most sacred mountain of the Canaanites.

4 When the kings joined forces,
  when they advanced together,
5 they saw her and were astounded;
  they fled in terror.
6 Trembling seized them there,
  pain like that of a woman in labor.
7 You destroyed them like ships of Tarshish
  shattered by an east wind.

8 As we have heard,
  so we have seen
 in the city of the LORD Almighty,
  in the city of our God:
 God makes her secure
  forever.*a*

9 Within your temple, O God,
  we meditate on your unfailing love.
10 Like your name, O God,
  your praise reaches to the ends of the earth;
  your right hand is filled with righteousness.
11 Mount Zion rejoices,
  the villages of Judah are glad
  because of your judgments.

12 Walk about Zion, go around her,
  count her towers,
13 consider well her ramparts,
  view her citadels,
 that you may tell of them
  to the next generation.

14 For this God is our God for ever and ever;
  he will be our guide even to the end.

Psalm 49*b*

For the director of music. Of the Sons of Korah. A psalm.

1 Hear this, all you peoples;
  listen, all who live in this world,
2 both low and high,
  rich and poor alike:
3 My mouth will speak words of wisdom;
  the meditation of my heart will give you understanding.
4 I will turn my ear to a proverb;
  with the harp I will expound my riddle:

5 Why should I fear when evil days come,
  when wicked deceivers surround me —

---

a 8 The Hebrew has *Selah* (a word of uncertain meaning) here.   *b* In Hebrew texts 49:1-20 is numbered 49:2-21.

⁶ those who trust in their wealth
    and boast of their great riches?
⁷ No one can redeem the life of another
    or give to God a ransom for them —
⁸ the ransom for a life is costly,
    no payment is ever enough —
⁹ so that they should live on forever
    and not see decay.
¹⁰ For all can see that the wise die,
    that the foolish and the senseless also perish,
    leaving their wealth to others.
¹¹ Their tombs will remain their houses*a* forever,
    their dwellings for endless generations,
    though they had*b* named lands after themselves.

¹² People, despite their wealth, do not endure;
    they are like the beasts that perish.

¹³ This is the fate of those who trust in themselves,
    and of their followers, who approve their sayings.*c*
¹⁴ They are like sheep and are destined to die;
    death will be their shepherd
    (but the upright will prevail over them in the morning).
  Their forms will decay in the grave,
    far from their princely mansions.
¹⁵ But God will redeem me from the realm of the dead;
    he will surely take me to himself.
¹⁶ Do not be overawed when others grow rich,
    when the splendor of their houses increases;
¹⁷ for they will take nothing with them when they die,
    their splendor will not descend with them.
¹⁸ Though while they live they count themselves blessed —
    and people praise you when you prosper —
¹⁹ they will join those who have gone before them,
    who will never again see the light of life.

²⁰ People who have wealth but lack understanding
    are like the beasts that perish.

Psalm 50

A psalm of Asaph.

¹ The Mighty One, God, the LORD,
    speaks and summons the earth
    from the rising of the sun to where it sets.
² From Zion, perfect in beauty,
    God shines forth.

---

a 11 Septuagint and Syriac; Hebrew *In their thoughts their houses will remain*   *b 11* Or *generations, / for they have*   *c 13* The Hebrew has *Selah* (a word of uncertain meaning) here and at the end of verse 15.

³ Our God comes
    and will not be silent;
  a fire devours before him,
    and around him a tempest rages.
⁴ He summons the heavens above,
    and the earth, that he may judge his people:
⁵ "Gather to me this consecrated people,
    who made a covenant with me by sacrifice."
⁶ And the heavens proclaim his righteousness,
    for he is a God of justice.ᵃ,ᵇ

⁷ "Listen, my people, and I will speak;
    I will testify against you, Israel:
    I am God, your God.
⁸ I bring no charges against you concerning your sacrifices
    or concerning your burnt offerings, which are ever before me.
⁹ I have no need of a bull from your stall
    or of goats from your pens,
¹⁰ for every animal of the forest is mine,
    and the cattle on a thousand hills.
¹¹ I know every bird in the mountains,
    and the insects in the fields are mine.
¹² If I were hungry I would not tell you,
    for the world is mine, and all that is in it.
¹³ Do I eat the flesh of bulls
    or drink the blood of goats?

¹⁴ "Sacrifice thank offerings to God,
    fulfill your vows to the Most High,
¹⁵ and call on me in the day of trouble;
    I will deliver you, and you will honor me."

¹⁶ But to the wicked person, God says:

"What right have you to recite my laws
    or take my covenant on your lips?
¹⁷ You hate my instruction
    and cast my words behind you.
¹⁸ When you see a thief, you join with him;
    you throw in your lot with adulterers.
¹⁹ You use your mouth for evil
    and harness your tongue to deceit.
²⁰ You sit and testify against your brother
    and slander your own mother's son.
²¹ When you did these things and I kept silent,
    you thought I was exactlyᶜ like you.
  But I now arraign you
    and set my accusations before you.

ᵃ 6 With a different word division of the Hebrew; Masoretic Text *for God himself is judge*   ᵇ 6 The Hebrew has *Selah* (a word of uncertain meaning) here.   ᶜ 21 Or *thought the 'I AM' was*

22 "Consider this, you who forget God,
   or I will tear you to pieces, with no one to rescue you:
23 Those who sacrifice thank offerings honor me,
   and to the blameless[a] I will show my salvation."

Psalm 51[b]

*For the director of music. A psalm of David. When the prophet Nathan
came to him after David had committed adultery with Bathsheba.*

1 Have mercy on me, O God,
   according to your unfailing love;
  according to your great compassion
   blot out my transgressions.
2 Wash away all my iniquity
   and cleanse me from my sin.

3 For I know my transgressions,
   and my sin is always before me.
4 Against you, you only, have I sinned
   and done what is evil in your sight;
  so you are right in your verdict
   and justified when you judge.
5 Surely I was sinful at birth,
   sinful from the time my mother conceived me.
6 Yet you desired faithfulness even in the womb;
   you taught me wisdom in that secret place.

7 Cleanse me with hyssop, and I will be clean;
   wash me, and I will be whiter than snow.
8 Let me hear joy and gladness;
   let the bones you have crushed rejoice.
9 Hide your face from my sins
   and blot out all my iniquity.

10 Create in me a pure heart, O God,
   and renew a steadfast spirit within me.
11 Do not cast me from your presence
   or take your Holy Spirit from me.
12 Restore to me the joy of your salvation
   and grant me a willing spirit, to sustain me.

13 Then I will teach transgressors your ways,
   so that sinners will turn back to you.
14 Deliver me from the guilt of bloodshed, O God,
   you who are God my Savior,
   and my tongue will sing of your righteousness.
15 Open my lips, Lord,
   and my mouth will declare your praise.

[a] 23 Probable reading of the original Hebrew text; the meaning of the Masoretic Text for this phrase is uncertain.   [b] In Hebrew texts 51:1-19 is numbered 51:3-21.

16 You do not delight in sacrifice, or I would bring it;
     you do not take pleasure in burnt offerings.
17 My sacrifice, O God, is*a* a broken spirit;
     a broken and contrite heart
     you, God, will not despise.

18 May it please you to prosper Zion,
     to build up the walls of Jerusalem.
19 Then you will delight in the sacrifices of the righteous,
     in burnt offerings offered whole;
     then bulls will be offered on your altar.

Psalm 52*b*

For the director of music. A maskil*c of David. When Doeg the Edomite had*
gone to Saul and told him: "David has gone to the house of Ahimelek."

1 Why do you boast of evil, you mighty hero?
     Why do you boast all day long,
     you who are a disgrace in the eyes of God?
2 You who practice deceit,
     your tongue plots destruction;
     it is like a sharpened razor.
3 You love evil rather than good,
     falsehood rather than speaking the truth.*d*
4 You love every harmful word,
     you deceitful tongue!

5 Surely God will bring you down to everlasting ruin:
     He will snatch you up and pluck you from your tent;
     he will uproot you from the land of the living.
6 The righteous will see and fear;
     they will laugh at you, saying,
7 "Here now is the man
     who did not make God his stronghold
 but trusted in his great wealth
     and grew strong by destroying others!"

8 But I am like an olive tree
     flourishing in the house of God;
 I trust in God's unfailing love
     for ever and ever.
9 For what you have done I will always praise you
     in the presence of your faithful people.
 And I will hope in your name,
     for your name is good.

---

a 17 Or *The sacrifices of God are*   *b* In Hebrew texts 52:1-9 is numbered 52:3-11.   *c* Title: Probably a literary or
musical term   *d 3* The Hebrew has *Selah* (a word of uncertain meaning) here and at the end of verse 5.

Psalm 53[a]

For the director of music. According to mahalath.[b] *A maskil[c] of David.*

[1] The fool says in his heart,
    "There is no God."
 They are corrupt, and their ways are vile;
    there is no one who does good.

[2] God looks down from heaven
    on all mankind
 to see if there are any who understand,
    any who seek God.
[3] Everyone has turned away, all have become corrupt;
    there is no one who does good,
        not even one.

[4] Do all these evildoers know nothing?

 They devour my people as though eating bread;
    they never call on God.
[5] But there they are, overwhelmed with dread,
    where there was nothing to dread.
 God scattered the bones of those who attacked you;
    you put them to shame, for God despised them.

[6] Oh, that salvation for Israel would come out of Zion!
    When God restores his people,
        let Jacob rejoice and Israel be glad!

Psalm 54[d]

*For the director of music. With stringed instruments. A maskil[c] of David. When
the Ziphites had gone to Saul and said, "Is not David hiding among us?"*

[1] Save me, O God, by your name;
    vindicate me by your might.
[2] Hear my prayer, O God;
    listen to the words of my mouth.

[3] Arrogant foes are attacking me;
    ruthless people are trying to kill me —
        people without regard for God.[e]

[4] Surely God is my help;
    the Lord is the one who sustains me.

[5] Let evil recoil on those who slander me;
    in your faithfulness destroy them.

---

[a] In Hebrew texts 53:1-6 is numbered 53:2-7.   [b] Title: Probably a musical term   [c] Title: Probably a literary or
musical term   [d] In Hebrew texts 54:1-7 is numbered 54:3-9.   [e] 3 The Hebrew has *Selah* (a word of
uncertain meaning) here.

⁶ I will sacrifice a freewill offering to you;
　　I will praise your name, LORD, for it is good.
⁷ You have delivered me from all my troubles,
　　and my eyes have looked in triumph on my foes.

Psalm 55ᵃ

For the director of music. With stringed instruments. A maskilᵇ *of David.*

¹ Listen to my prayer, O God,
　　do not ignore my plea;
²　hear me and answer me.
　My thoughts trouble me and I am distraught
³　because of what my enemy is saying,
　　because of the threats of the wicked;
　for they bring down suffering on me
　　and assail me in their anger.

⁴ My heart is in anguish within me;
　　the terrors of death have fallen on me.
⁵ Fear and trembling have beset me;
　　horror has overwhelmed me.
⁶ I said, "Oh, that I had the wings of a dove!
　　I would fly away and be at rest.
⁷ I would flee far away
　　and stay in the desert;ᶜ
⁸ I would hurry to my place of shelter,
　　far from the tempest and storm."

⁹ Lord, confuse the wicked, confound their words,
　　for I see violence and strife in the city.
¹⁰ Day and night they prowl about on its walls;
　　malice and abuse are within it.
¹¹ Destructive forces are at work in the city;
　　threats and lies never leave its streets.

¹² If an enemy were insulting me,
　　I could endure it;
　if a foe were rising against me,
　　I could hide.
¹³ But it is you, a man like myself,
　　my companion, my close friend,
¹⁴ with whom I once enjoyed sweet fellowship
　　at the house of God,
　as we walked about
　　among the worshipers.

¹⁵ Let death take my enemies by surprise;
　　let them go down alive to the realm of the dead,
　　for evil finds lodging among them.

ᵃ In Hebrew texts 55:1-23 is numbered 55:2-24.　　ᵇ Title: Probably a literary or musical term　　ᶜ 7 The Hebrew has *Selah* (a word of uncertain meaning) here and in the middle of verse 19.

¹⁶As for me, I call to God,
 and the LORD saves me.
¹⁷Evening, morning and noon
 I cry out in distress,
 and he hears my voice.
¹⁸He rescues me unharmed
 from the battle waged against me,
 even though many oppose me.
¹⁹God, who is enthroned from of old,
 who does not change —
he will hear them and humble them,
 because they have no fear of God.

²⁰My companion attacks his friends;
 he violates his covenant.
²¹His talk is smooth as butter,
 yet war is in his heart;
his words are more soothing than oil,
 yet they are drawn swords.

²²Cast your cares on the LORD
 and he will sustain you;
he will never let
 the righteous be shaken.
²³But you, God, will bring down the wicked
 into the pit of decay;
the bloodthirsty and deceitful
 will not live out half their days.

But as for me, I trust in you.

Psalm 56[a]

For the director of music. To the tune of "A Dove on Distant Oaks." Of David.
A miktam.[b] When the Philistines had seized him in Gath.

¹Be merciful to me, my God,
 for my enemies are in hot pursuit;
 all day long they press their attack.
²My adversaries pursue me all day long;
 in their pride many are attacking me.

³When I am afraid, I put my trust in you.
⁴ In God, whose word I praise —
 in God I trust and am not afraid.
 What can mere mortals do to me?

⁵All day long they twist my words;
 all their schemes are for my ruin.
⁶They conspire, they lurk,
 they watch my steps,
 hoping to take my life.

---

[a] In Hebrew texts 56:1-13 is numbered 56:2-14.   [b] Title: Probably a literary or musical term

⁷ Because of their wickedness do not*ᵃ* let them escape;
   in your anger, God, bring the nations down.

⁸ Record my misery;
   list my tears on your scroll*ᵇ* —
   are they not in your record?
⁹ Then my enemies will turn back
   when I call for help.
   By this I will know that God is for me.

¹⁰ In God, whose word I praise,
   in the Lᴏʀᴅ, whose word I praise —
¹¹ in God I trust and am not afraid.
   What can man do to me?

¹² I am under vows to you, my God;
   I will present my thank offerings to you.
¹³ For you have delivered me from death
   and my feet from stumbling,
  that I may walk before God
   in the light of life.

Psalm 57*ᶜ*

*For the director of music. To the tune of "Do Not Destroy." Of David.
A miktam.*ᵈ* When he had fled from Saul into the cave.*

¹ Have mercy on me, my God, have mercy on me,
   for in you I take refuge.
 I will take refuge in the shadow of your wings
   until the disaster has passed.

² I cry out to God Most High,
   to God, who vindicates me.
³ He sends from heaven and saves me,
   rebuking those who hotly pursue me — *ᵉ*
   God sends forth his love and his faithfulness.

⁴ I am in the midst of lions;
   I am forced to dwell among ravenous beasts —
  men whose teeth are spears and arrows,
   whose tongues are sharp swords.

⁵ Be exalted, O God, above the heavens;
   let your glory be over all the earth.

⁶ They spread a net for my feet —
   I was bowed down in distress.
 They dug a pit in my path —
   but they have fallen into it themselves.

ᵃ 7 Probable reading of the original Hebrew text; Masoretic Text does not have *do not.*   *ᵇ 8* Or *misery; / put my tears in your wineskin*   *ᶜ* In Hebrew texts 57:1-11 is numbered 57:2-12.   *ᵈ Title:* Probably a literary or musical term   *ᵉ 3* The Hebrew has *Selah* (a word of uncertain meaning) here and at the end of verse 6.

7 My heart, O God, is steadfast,
   my heart is steadfast;
   I will sing and make music.
8 Awake, my soul!
   Awake, harp and lyre!
   I will awaken the dawn.

9 I will praise you, Lord, among the nations;
   I will sing of you among the peoples.
10 For great is your love, reaching to the heavens;
   your faithfulness reaches to the skies.

11 Be exalted, O God, above the heavens;
   let your glory be over all the earth.

Psalm 58 [a]

For the director of music. To the tune of "Do Not Destroy." Of David. A miktam. [b]

1 Do you rulers indeed speak justly?
   Do you judge people with equity?
2 No, in your heart you devise injustice,
   and your hands mete out violence on the earth.

3 Even from birth the wicked go astray;
   from the womb they are wayward, spreading lies.
4 Their venom is like the venom of a snake,
   like that of a cobra that has stopped its ears,
5 that will not heed the tune of the charmer,
   however skillful the enchanter may be.

6 Break the teeth in their mouths, O God;
   LORD, tear out the fangs of those lions!
7 Let them vanish like water that flows away;
   when they draw the bow, let their arrows fall short.
8 May they be like a slug that melts away as it moves along,
   like a stillborn child that never sees the sun.

9 Before your pots can feel the heat of the thorns —
   whether they be green or dry — the wicked will be swept away. [c]
10 The righteous will be glad when they are avenged,
   when they dip their feet in the blood of the wicked.
11 Then people will say,
   "Surely the righteous still are rewarded;
   surely there is a God who judges the earth."

---

[a] In Hebrew texts 58:1-11 is numbered 58:2-12.   [b] Title: Probably a literary or musical term   [c] 9 The meaning of the Hebrew for this verse is uncertain.

Psalm 59[a]

For the director of music. To the tune of "Do Not Destroy." Of David. A miktam.[b]
When Saul had sent men to watch David's house in order to kill him.

[1] Deliver me from my enemies, O God;
    be my fortress against those who are attacking me.
[2] Deliver me from evildoers
    and save me from those who are after my blood.

[3] See how they lie in wait for me!
    Fierce men conspire against me
    for no offense or sin of mine, LORD.
[4] I have done no wrong, yet they are ready to attack me.
    Arise to help me; look on my plight!
[5] You, LORD God Almighty,
    you who are the God of Israel,
  rouse yourself to punish all the nations;
    show no mercy to wicked traitors.[c]

[6] They return at evening,
    snarling like dogs,
    and prowl about the city.
[7] See what they spew from their mouths —
    the words from their lips are sharp as swords,
    and they think, "Who can hear us?"
[8] But you laugh at them, LORD;
    you scoff at all those nations.

[9] You are my strength, I watch for you;
    you, God, are my fortress,
[10]   my God on whom I can rely.

  God will go before me
    and will let me gloat over those who slander me.
[11] But do not kill them, Lord our shield,[d]
    or my people will forget.
  In your might uproot them
    and bring them down.
[12] For the sins of their mouths,
    for the words of their lips,
    let them be caught in their pride.
  For the curses and lies they utter,
[13]   consume them in your wrath,
    consume them till they are no more.
  Then it will be known to the ends of the earth
    that God rules over Jacob.

---

[a] In Hebrew texts 59:1-17 is numbered 59:2-18.   [b] Title: Probably a literary or musical term   [c] 5 The Hebrew has Selah *(a word of uncertain meaning) here and at the end of verse 13.   [d] 11 Or* sovereign

14 They return at evening,
    snarling like dogs,
    and prowl about the city.
15 They wander about for food
    and howl if not satisfied.
16 But I will sing of your strength,
    in the morning I will sing of your love;
  for you are my fortress,
    my refuge in times of trouble.

17 You are my strength, I sing praise to you;
    you, God, are my fortress,
    my God on whom I can rely.

Psalm 60[a]

For the director of music. To the tune of "The Lily of the Covenant." A miktam[b] of David.
For teaching. When he fought Aram Naharaim[c] and Aram Zobah,[d] and when Joab
returned and struck down twelve thousand Edomites in the Valley of Salt.

1 You have rejected us, God, and burst upon us;
    you have been angry — now restore us!
2 You have shaken the land and torn it open;
    mend its fractures, for it is quaking.
3 You have shown your people desperate times;
    you have given us wine that makes us stagger.
4 But for those who fear you, you have raised a banner
    to be unfurled against the bow.[e]

5 Save us and help us with your right hand,
    that those you love may be delivered.
6 God has spoken from his sanctuary:
    "In triumph I will parcel out Shechem
    and measure off the Valley of Sukkoth.
7 Gilead is mine, and Manasseh is mine;
    Ephraim is my helmet,
    Judah is my scepter.
8 Moab is my washbasin,
    on Edom I toss my sandal;
    over Philistia I shout in triumph."

9 Who will bring me to the fortified city?
    Who will lead me to Edom?
10 Is it not you, God, you who have now rejected us
    and no longer go out with our armies?
11 Give us aid against the enemy,
    for human help is worthless.
12 With God we will gain the victory,
    and he will trample down our enemies.

---

[a] In Hebrew texts 60:1-12 is numbered 60:3-14.   [b] Title: Probably a literary or musical term   [c] Title: That is,
Arameans of Northwest Mesopotamia   [d] Title: That is, Arameans of central Syria   [e] 4 The Hebrew has
Selah (a word of uncertain meaning) here.

Psalm 61[a]

For the director of music. With stringed instruments. Of David.

[1] Hear my cry, O God;
    listen to my prayer.

[2] From the ends of the earth I call to you,
    I call as my heart grows faint;
    lead me to the rock that is higher than I.
[3] For you have been my refuge,
    a strong tower against the foe.

[4] I long to dwell in your tent forever
    and take refuge in the shelter of your wings.[b]
[5] For you, God, have heard my vows;
    you have given me the heritage of those who fear your name.

[6] Increase the days of the king's life,
    his years for many generations.
[7] May he be enthroned in God's presence forever;
    appoint your love and faithfulness to protect him.

[8] Then I will ever sing in praise of your name
    and fulfill my vows day after day.

Psalm 62[c]

For the director of music. For Jeduthun. A psalm of David.

[1] Truly my soul finds rest in God;
    my salvation comes from him.
[2] Truly he is my rock and my salvation;
    he is my fortress, I will never be shaken.

[3] How long will you assault me?
    Would all of you throw me down —
    this leaning wall, this tottering fence?
[4] Surely they intend to topple me
    from my lofty place;
    they take delight in lies.
  With their mouths they bless,
    but in their hearts they curse.[d]

[5] Yes, my soul, find rest in God;
    my hope comes from him.
[6] Truly he is my rock and my salvation;
    he is my fortress, I will not be shaken.
[7] My salvation and my honor depend on God[e];
    he is my mighty rock, my refuge.

---

[a] In Hebrew texts 61:1-8 is numbered 61:2-9.   [b] 4 The Hebrew has *Selah* (a word of uncertain meaning) here.
[c] In Hebrew texts 62:1-12 is numbered 62:2-13.   [d] 4 The Hebrew has *Selah* (a word of uncertain meaning) here
and at the end of verse 8.   [e] 7 Or / *God Most High is my salvation and my honor*

_____

_____

_____

_____

_____

_____

_____

_____

_____

_____

_____

_____

_____

_____

_____

_____

_____

_____

_____

Life in Bible Times

What God Is Like

Psalm 61:3 says that God is like a strong tower. Strong towers were built inside walled cities. Even if the walls were broken down, the people of the city would be safe inside the tower.

8 Trust in him at all times, you people;
    pour out your hearts to him,
    for God is our refuge.

9 Surely the lowborn are but a breath,
    the highborn are but a lie.
  If weighed on a balance, they are nothing;
    together they are only a breath.
10 Do not trust in extortion
    or put vain hope in stolen goods;
  though your riches increase,
    do not set your heart on them.

11 One thing God has spoken,
    two things I have heard:
  "Power belongs to you, God,
12   and with you, Lord, is unfailing love";
  and, "You reward everyone
    according to what they have done."

Psalm 63[a]

A psalm of David. When he was in the Desert of Judah.

1 You, God, are my God,
    earnestly I seek you;
  I thirst for you,
    my whole being longs for you,
  in a dry and parched land
    where there is no water.

2 I have seen you in the sanctuary
    and beheld your power and your glory.
3 Because your love is better than life,
    my lips will glorify you.
4 I will praise you as long as I live,
    and in your name I will lift up my hands.
5 I will be fully satisfied as with the richest of foods;
    with singing lips my mouth will praise you.

6 On my bed I remember you;
    I think of you through the watches of the night.
7 Because you are my help,
    I sing in the shadow of your wings.
8 I cling to you;
    your right hand upholds me.

9 Those who want to kill me will be destroyed;
    they will go down to the depths of the earth.
10 They will be given over to the sword
    and become food for jackals.

a In Hebrew texts 63:1-11 is numbered 63:2-12.

11 But the king will rejoice in God;
    all who swear by God will glory in him,
    while the mouths of liars will be silenced.

Psalm 64 [a]

For the director of music. A psalm of David.

1 Hear me, my God, as I voice my complaint;
    protect my life from the threat of the enemy.

2 Hide me from the conspiracy of the wicked,
    from the plots of evildoers.
3 They sharpen their tongues like swords
    and aim cruel words like deadly arrows.
4 They shoot from ambush at the innocent;
    they shoot suddenly, without fear.

5 They encourage each other in evil plans,
    they talk about hiding their snares;
    they say, "Who will see it [b]?"
6 They plot injustice and say,
    "We have devised a perfect plan!"
    Surely the human mind and heart are cunning.

7 But God will shoot them with his arrows;
    they will suddenly be struck down.
8 He will turn their own tongues against them
    and bring them to ruin;
    all who see them will shake their heads in scorn.
9 All people will fear;
    they will proclaim the works of God
    and ponder what he has done.

10 The righteous will rejoice in the Lord
    and take refuge in him;
    all the upright in heart will glory in him!

Psalm 65 [c]

For the director of music. A psalm of David. A song.

1 Praise awaits [d] you, our God, in Zion;
    to you our vows will be fulfilled.
2 You who answer prayer,
    to you all people will come.
3 When we were overwhelmed by sins,
    you forgave [e] our transgressions.
4 Blessed are those you choose
    and bring near to live in your courts!

---

[a] In Hebrew texts 64:1-10 is numbered 64:2-11.   [b] 5 Or *us*   [c] In Hebrew texts 65:1-13 is numbered 65:2-14.
[d] 1 Or *befits*; the meaning of the Hebrew for this word is uncertain.   [e] 3 Or *made atonement for*

Lying Awake at Night

Do you have a hard time going to sleep sometimes? This psalm tells what David did when he couldn't get to sleep. Read Psalm 63:6–8 and try these things when lying awake:

1. Remember Bible stories and things God has done for people.
2. Quietly sing some songs about God.
3. Snuggle down in your blankets, close your eyes, and, as you feel the warmth, remember that God is close to you and he loves you.

Psalm 63:6–8

We are filled with the good things of your house,
   of your holy temple.

5 You answer us with awesome and righteous deeds,
   God our Savior,
 the hope of all the ends of the earth
   and of the farthest seas,
6 who formed the mountains by your power,
   having armed yourself with strength,
7 who stilled the roaring of the seas,
   the roaring of their waves,
   and the turmoil of the nations.
8 The whole earth is filled with awe at your wonders;
   where morning dawns, where evening fades,
   you call forth songs of joy.

9 You care for the land and water it;
   you enrich it abundantly.
 The streams of God are filled with water
   to provide the people with grain,
   for so you have ordained it.*a*
10 You drench its furrows and level its ridges;
   you soften it with showers and bless its crops.
11 You crown the year with your bounty,
   and your carts overflow with abundance.
12 The grasslands of the wilderness overflow;
   the hills are clothed with gladness.
13 The meadows are covered with flocks
   and the valleys are mantled with grain;
   they shout for joy and sing.

Psalm 66

For the director of music. A song. A psalm.

1 Shout for joy to God, all the earth!
2   Sing the glory of his name;
   make his praise glorious.
3 Say to God, "How awesome are your deeds!
   So great is your power
   that your enemies cringe before you.
4 All the earth bows down to you;
   they sing praise to you,
   they sing the praises of your name."*b*

5 Come and see what God has done,
   his awesome deeds for mankind!
6 He turned the sea into dry land,
   they passed through the waters on foot —
   come, let us rejoice in him.

---

a 9 Or *for that is how you prepare the land*   *b* 4 The Hebrew has *Selah* (a word of uncertain meaning) here
and at the end of verses 7 and 15.

7 He rules forever by his power,
his eyes watch the nations —
let not the rebellious rise up against him.

8 Praise our God, all peoples,
let the sound of his praise be heard;
9 he has preserved our lives
and kept our feet from slipping.
10 For you, God, tested us;
you refined us like silver.
11 You brought us into prison
and laid burdens on our backs.
12 You let people ride over our heads;
we went through fire and water,
but you brought us to a place of abundance.

13 I will come to your temple with burnt offerings
and fulfill my vows to you —
14 vows my lips promised and my mouth spoke
when I was in trouble.
15 I will sacrifice fat animals to you
and an offering of rams;
I will offer bulls and goats.

16 Come and hear, all you who fear God;
let me tell you what he has done for me.
17 I cried out to him with my mouth;
his praise was on my tongue.
18 If I had cherished sin in my heart,
the Lord would not have listened;
19 but God has surely listened
and has heard my prayer.
20 Praise be to God,
who has not rejected my prayer
or withheld his love from me!

Psalm 67[a]

For the director of music. With stringed instruments. A psalm. A song.

1 May God be gracious to us and bless us
and make his face shine on us — [b]
2 so that your ways may be known on earth,
your salvation among all nations.

3 May the peoples praise you, God;
may all the peoples praise you.
4 May the nations be glad and sing for joy,
for you rule the peoples with equity
and guide the nations of the earth.

[a] In Hebrew texts 67:1-7 is numbered 67:2-8.   [b] 1 The Hebrew has *Selah* (a word of uncertain meaning) here and at the end of verse 4.

⁵ May the peoples praise you, God;
    may all the peoples praise you.

⁶ The land yields its harvest;
    God, our God, blesses us.
⁷ May God bless us still,
    so that all the ends of the earth will fear him.

Psalm 68[a]

For the director of music. Of David. A psalm. A song.

¹ May God arise, may his enemies be scattered;
    may his foes flee before him.
² May you blow them away like smoke —
    as wax melts before the fire,
    may the wicked perish before God.
³ But may the righteous be glad
    and rejoice before God;
    may they be happy and joyful.

⁴ Sing to God, sing in praise of his name,
    extol him who rides on the clouds[b];
    rejoice before him — his name is the LORD.
⁵ A father to the fatherless, a defender of widows,
    is God in his holy dwelling.
⁶ God sets the lonely in families,[c]
    he leads out the prisoners with singing;
    but the rebellious live in a sun-scorched land.

⁷ When you, God, went out before your people,
    when you marched through the wilderness,[d]
⁸ the earth shook, the heavens poured down rain,
    before God, the One of Sinai,
    before God, the God of Israel.
⁹ You gave abundant showers, O God;
    you refreshed your weary inheritance.
¹⁰ Your people settled in it,
    and from your bounty, God, you provided for the poor.

¹¹ The Lord announces the word,
    and the women who proclaim it are a mighty throng:
¹² "Kings and armies flee in haste;
    the women at home divide the plunder.
¹³ Even while you sleep among the sheep pens,[e]
    the wings of my dove are sheathed with silver,
    its feathers with shining gold."
¹⁴ When the Almighty[f] scattered the kings in the land,
    it was like snow fallen on Mount Zalmon.

ᵃ In Hebrew texts 68:1-35 is numbered 68:2-36.   ᵇ 4 Or name, / prepare the way for him who rides through the deserts   ᶜ 6 Or the desolate in a homeland   ᵈ 7 The Hebrew has Selah (a word of uncertain meaning) here and at the end of verses 19 and 32.   ᵉ 13 Or the campfires; or the saddlebags   ᶠ 14 Hebrew Shaddai

¹⁵ Mount Bashan, majestic mountain,
    Mount Bashan, rugged mountain,
¹⁶ why gaze in envy, you rugged mountain,
    at the mountain where God chooses to reign,
    where the LORD himself will dwell forever?
¹⁷ The chariots of God are tens of thousands
    and thousands of thousands;
    the Lord has come from Sinai into his sanctuary.ᵃ
¹⁸ When you ascended on high,
    you took many captives;
    you received gifts from people,
  even fromᵇ the rebellious —
    that you,ᶜ LORD God, might dwell there.

¹⁹ Praise be to the Lord, to God our Savior,
    who daily bears our burdens.
²⁰ Our God is a God who saves;
    from the Sovereign LORD comes escape from death.
²¹ Surely God will crush the heads of his enemies,
    the hairy crowns of those who go on in their sins.
²² The Lord says, "I will bring them from Bashan;
    I will bring them from the depths of the sea,
²³ that your feet may wade in the blood of your foes,
    while the tongues of your dogs have their share."

²⁴ Your procession, God, has come into view,
    the procession of my God and King into the sanctuary.
²⁵ In front are the singers, after them the musicians;
    with them are the young women playing the timbrels.
²⁶ Praise God in the great congregation;
    praise the LORD in the assembly of Israel.
²⁷ There is the little tribe of Benjamin, leading them,
    there the great throng of Judah's princes,
    and there the princes of Zebulun and of Naphtali.

²⁸ Summon your power, Godᵈ;
    show us your strength, our God, as you have done before.
²⁹ Because of your temple at Jerusalem
    kings will bring you gifts.
³⁰ Rebuke the beast among the reeds,
    the herd of bulls among the calves of the nations.
  Humbled, may the beast bring bars of silver.
    Scatter the nations who delight in war.
³¹ Envoys will come from Egypt;
    Cushᵉ will submit herself to God.

ᵃ 17 Probable reading of the original Hebrew text; Masoretic Text Lord is among them at Sinai in holiness
ᵇ 18 Or gifts for people, / even   ᶜ 18 Or they   ᵈ 28 Many Hebrew manuscripts, Septuagint and Syriac; most
Hebrew manuscripts Your God has summoned power for you   ᵉ 31 That is, the upper Nile region

³²Sing to God, you kingdoms of the earth,
    sing praise to the Lord,
³³to him who rides across the highest heavens, the ancient heavens,
    who thunders with mighty voice.
³⁴Proclaim the power of God,
    whose majesty is over Israel,
    whose power is in the heavens.
³⁵You, God, are awesome in your sanctuary;
    the God of Israel gives power and strength to his people.

Praise be to God!

Psalm 69[a]

For the director of music. To the tune of "Lilies." Of David.

¹Save me, O God,
    for the waters have come up to my neck.
²I sink in the miry depths,
    where there is no foothold.
I have come into the deep waters;
    the floods engulf me.
³I am worn out calling for help;
    my throat is parched.
My eyes fail,
    looking for my God.
⁴Those who hate me without reason
    outnumber the hairs of my head;
many are my enemies without cause,
    those who seek to destroy me.
I am forced to restore
    what I did not steal.

⁵You, God, know my folly;
    my guilt is not hidden from you.

⁶Lord, the LORD Almighty,
    may those who hope in you
    not be disgraced because of me;
God of Israel,
    may those who seek you
    not be put to shame because of me.
⁷For I endure scorn for your sake,
    and shame covers my face.
⁸I am a foreigner to my own family,
    a stranger to my own mother's children;
⁹for zeal for your house consumes me,
    and the insults of those who insult you fall on me.
¹⁰When I weep and fast,
    I must endure scorn;

---

[a] In Hebrew texts 69:1-36 is numbered 69:2-37.

11 when I put on sackcloth,
  people make sport of me.
12 Those who sit at the gate mock me,
  and I am the song of the drunkards.

13 But I pray to you, LORD,
  in the time of your favor;
 in your great love, O God,
  answer me with your sure salvation.
14 Rescue me from the mire,
  do not let me sink;
 deliver me from those who hate me,
  from the deep waters.
15 Do not let the floodwaters engulf me
  or the depths swallow me up
  or the pit close its mouth over me.

16 Answer me, LORD, out of the goodness of your love;
  in your great mercy turn to me.
17 Do not hide your face from your servant;
  answer me quickly, for I am in trouble.
18 Come near and rescue me;
  deliver me because of my foes.

19 You know how I am scorned, disgraced and shamed;
  all my enemies are before you.
20 Scorn has broken my heart
  and has left me helpless;
 I looked for sympathy, but there was none,
  for comforters, but I found none.
21 They put gall in my food
  and gave me vinegar for my thirst.

22 May the table set before them become a snare;
  may it become retribution and*a* a trap.
23 May their eyes be darkened so they cannot see,
  and their backs be bent forever.
24 Pour out your wrath on them;
  let your fierce anger overtake them.
25 May their place be deserted;
  let there be no one to dwell in their tents.
26 For they persecute those you wound
  and talk about the pain of those you hurt.
27 Charge them with crime upon crime;
  do not let them share in your salvation.
28 May they be blotted out of the book of life
  and not be listed with the righteous.

29 But as for me, afflicted and in pain —
  may your salvation, God, protect me.

a 22 Or snare / and their fellowship become

³⁰ I will praise God's name in song
     and glorify him with thanksgiving.
³¹ This will please the LORD more than an ox,
     more than a bull with its horns and hooves.
³² The poor will see and be glad —
     you who seek God, may your hearts live!
³³ The LORD hears the needy
     and does not despise his captive people.

³⁴ Let heaven and earth praise him,
     the seas and all that move in them,
³⁵ for God will save Zion
     and rebuild the cities of Judah.
   Then people will settle there and possess it;
³⁶   the children of his servants will inherit it,
     and those who love his name will dwell there.

Psalm 70ᵃ

For the director of music. Of David. A petition.

¹ Hasten, O God, to save me;
     come quickly, LORD, to help me.

² May those who want to take my life
     be put to shame and confusion;
   may all who desire my ruin
     be turned back in disgrace.
³ May those who say to me, "Aha! Aha!"
     turn back because of their shame.
⁴ But may all who seek you
     rejoice and be glad in you;
   may those who long for your saving help always say,
     "The LORD is great!"

⁵ But as for me, I am poor and needy;
     come quickly to me, O God.
   You are my help and my deliverer;
     LORD, do not delay.

Psalm 71

¹ In you, LORD, I have taken refuge;
     let me never be put to shame.
² In your righteousness, rescue me and deliver me;
     turn your ear to me and save me.
³ Be my rock of refuge,
     to which I can always go;
   give the command to save me,
     for you are my rock and my fortress.

ᵃ In Hebrew texts 70:1-5 is numbered 70:2-6.

Life in Bible Times

What God Is Like

Psalm 71:3 says that God is a rock of refuge. Some cities and forts were built on high, rocky mountain cliffs. It was extremely difficult for enemies to attack such cities. To call God a rock of refuge means that we are safest when we trust in him.

[4] Deliver me, my God, from the hand of the wicked,
  from the grasp of those who are evil and cruel.

[5] For you have been my hope, Sovereign LORD,
    my confidence since my youth.
[6] From birth I have relied on you;
    you brought me forth from my mother's womb.
    I will ever praise you.
[7] I have become a sign to many;
    you are my strong refuge.
[8] My mouth is filled with your praise,
    declaring your splendor all day long.

[9] Do not cast me away when I am old;
    do not forsake me when my strength is gone.
[10] For my enemies speak against me;
    those who wait to kill me conspire together.
[11] They say, "God has forsaken him;
    pursue him and seize him,
    for no one will rescue him."
[12] Do not be far from me, my God;
    come quickly, God, to help me.
[13] May my accusers perish in shame;
    may those who want to harm me
    be covered with scorn and disgrace.

[14] As for me, I will always have hope;
    I will praise you more and more.

[15] My mouth will tell of your righteous deeds,
    of your saving acts all day long —
    though I know not how to relate them all.
[16] I will come and proclaim your mighty acts, Sovereign LORD;
    I will proclaim your righteous deeds, yours alone.
[17] Since my youth, God, you have taught me,
    and to this day I declare your marvelous deeds.
[18] Even when I am old and gray,
    do not forsake me, my God,
  till I declare your power to the next generation,
    your mighty acts to all who are to come.

[19] Your righteousness, God, reaches to the heavens,
    you who have done great things.
    Who is like you, God?
[20] Though you have made me see troubles,
    many and bitter,
    you will restore my life again;
  from the depths of the earth
    you will again bring me up.
[21] You will increase my honor
    and comfort me once more.

22 I will praise you with the harp
for your faithfulness, my God;
I will sing praise to you with the lyre,
Holy One of Israel.
23 My lips will shout for joy
when I sing praise to you —
I whom you have delivered.
24 My tongue will tell of your righteous acts
all day long,
for those who wanted to harm me
have been put to shame and confusion.

Psalm 72

Of Solomon.

1 Endow the king with your justice, O God,
the royal son with your righteousness.
2 May he judge your people in righteousness,
your afflicted ones with justice.

3 May the mountains bring prosperity to the people,
the hills the fruit of righteousness.
4 May he defend the afflicted among the people
and save the children of the needy;
may he crush the oppressor.
5 May he endure[a] as long as the sun,
as long as the moon, through all generations.
6 May he be like rain falling on a mown field,
like showers watering the earth.
7 In his days may the righteous flourish
and prosperity abound till the moon is no more.

8 May he rule from sea to sea
and from the River[b] to the ends of the earth.
9 May the desert tribes bow before him
and his enemies lick the dust.
10 May the kings of Tarshish and of distant shores
bring tribute to him.
May the kings of Sheba and Seba
present him gifts.
11 May all kings bow down to him
and all nations serve him.

12 For he will deliver the needy who cry out,
the afflicted who have no one to help.
13 He will take pity on the weak and the needy
and save the needy from death.
14 He will rescue them from oppression and violence,
for precious is their blood in his sight.

---

a 5 Septuagint; Hebrew *You will be feared*   *b 8* That is, the Euphrates

¹⁵ Long may he live!
  May gold from Sheba be given him.
  May people ever pray for him
  and bless him all day long.
¹⁶ May grain abound throughout the land;
  on the tops of the hills may it sway.
  May the crops flourish like Lebanon
  and thrive*ᵃ* like the grass of the field.
¹⁷ May his name endure forever;
  may it continue as long as the sun.

  Then all nations will be blessed through him,*ᵇ*
  and they will call him blessed.

¹⁸ Praise be to the LORD God, the God of Israel,
  who alone does marvelous deeds.
¹⁹ Praise be to his glorious name forever;
  may the whole earth be filled with his glory.
                    Amen and Amen.

²⁰ This concludes the prayers of David son of Jesse.

BOOK III

Psalms 73 - 89

Psalm 73

A psalm of Asaph.

¹ Surely God is good to Israel,
  to those who are pure in heart.

² But as for me, my feet had almost slipped;
  I had nearly lost my foothold.
³ For I envied the arrogant
  when I saw the prosperity of the wicked.

⁴ They have no struggles;
  their bodies are healthy and strong.*ᶜ*
⁵ They are free from common human burdens;
  they are not plagued by human ills.
⁶ Therefore pride is their necklace;
  they clothe themselves with violence.
⁷ From their callous hearts comes iniquity*ᵈ*;
  their evil imaginations have no limits.

ᵃ 16 Probable reading of the original Hebrew text; Masoretic Text *Lebanon, / from the city*   *ᵇ* 17 Or *will use his name in blessings* (see Gen. 48:20)   *ᶜ* 4 With a different word division of the Hebrew; Masoretic Text *struggles at their death; / their bodies are healthy*   *ᵈ* 7 Syriac (see also Septuagint); Hebrew *Their eyes bulge with fat*

8 They scoff, and speak with malice;
    with arrogance they threaten oppression.
9 Their mouths lay claim to heaven,
    and their tongues take possession of the earth.
10 Therefore their people turn to them
    and drink up waters in abundance.[a]
11 They say, "How would God know?
    Does the Most High know anything?"

12 This is what the wicked are like —
    always free of care, they go on amassing wealth.

13 Surely in vain I have kept my heart pure
    and have washed my hands in innocence.
14 All day long I have been afflicted,
    and every morning brings new punishments.

15 If I had spoken out like that,
    I would have betrayed your children.
16 When I tried to understand all this,
    it troubled me deeply
17 till I entered the sanctuary of God;
    then I understood their final destiny.

18 Surely you place them on slippery ground;
    you cast them down to ruin.
19 How suddenly are they destroyed,
    completely swept away by terrors!
20 They are like a dream when one awakes;
    when you arise, Lord,
    you will despise them as fantasies.

21 When my heart was grieved
    and my spirit embittered,
22 I was senseless and ignorant;
    I was a brute beast before you.

23 Yet I am always with you;
    you hold me by my right hand.
24 You guide me with your counsel,
    and afterward you will take me into glory.
25 Whom have I in heaven but you?
    And earth has nothing I desire besides you.
26 My flesh and my heart may fail,
    but God is the strength of my heart
    and my portion forever.

27 Those who are far from you will perish;
    you destroy all who are unfaithful to you.
28 But as for me, it is good to be near God.
    I have made the Sovereign LORD my refuge;
    I will tell of all your deeds.

---

[a] 10 The meaning of the Hebrew for this verse is uncertain.

Psalm 74

A maskil[a] of Asaph.

1 O God, why have you rejected us forever?
　Why does your anger smolder against the sheep of your pasture?
2 Remember the nation you purchased long ago,
　the people of your inheritance, whom you redeemed —
　Mount Zion, where you dwelt.
3 Turn your steps toward these everlasting ruins,
　all this destruction the enemy has brought on the sanctuary.

4 Your foes roared in the place where you met with us;
　they set up their standards as signs.
5 They behaved like men wielding axes
　to cut through a thicket of trees.
6 They smashed all the carved paneling
　with their axes and hatchets.
7 They burned your sanctuary to the ground;
　they defiled the dwelling place of your Name.
8 They said in their hearts, "We will crush them completely!"
　They burned every place where God was worshiped in the land.

9 We are given no signs from God;
　no prophets are left,
　and none of us knows how long this will be.
10 How long will the enemy mock you, God?
　Will the foe revile your name forever?
11 Why do you hold back your hand, your right hand?
　Take it from the folds of your garment and destroy them!

12 But God is my King from long ago;
　he brings salvation on the earth.

13 It was you who split open the sea by your power;
　you broke the heads of the monster in the waters.
14 It was you who crushed the heads of Leviathan
　and gave it as food to the creatures of the desert.
15 It was you who opened up springs and streams;
　you dried up the ever-flowing rivers.
16 The day is yours, and yours also the night;
　you established the sun and moon.
17 It was you who set all the boundaries of the earth;
　you made both summer and winter.

18 Remember how the enemy has mocked you, LORD,
　how foolish people have reviled your name.
19 Do not hand over the life of your dove to wild beasts;
　do not forget the lives of your afflicted people forever.
20 Have regard for your covenant,
　because haunts of violence fill the dark places of the land.

---

a Title: Probably a literary or musical term

²¹Do not let the oppressed retreat in disgrace;
　　may the poor and needy praise your name.
²²Rise up, O God, and defend your cause;
　　remember how fools mock you all day long.
²³Do not ignore the clamor of your adversaries,
　　the uproar of your enemies, which rises continually.

Psalm 75[a]

For the director of music. To the tune of "Do Not Destroy." A psalm of Asaph. A song.

¹We praise you, God,
　　we praise you, for your Name is near;
　　people tell of your wonderful deeds.

²You say, "I choose the appointed time;
　　it is I who judge with equity.
³When the earth and all its people quake,
　　it is I who hold its pillars firm.[b]
⁴To the arrogant I say, 'Boast no more,'
　　and to the wicked, 'Do not lift up your horns.[c]
⁵Do not lift your horns against heaven;
　　do not speak so defiantly.'"

⁶No one from the east or the west
　　or from the desert can exalt themselves.
⁷It is God who judges:
　　He brings one down, he exalts another.
⁸In the hand of the LORD is a cup
　　full of foaming wine mixed with spices;
　he pours it out, and all the wicked of the earth
　　drink it down to its very dregs.

⁹As for me, I will declare this forever;
　　I will sing praise to the God of Jacob,
¹⁰who says, "I will cut off the horns of all the wicked,
　　but the horns of the righteous will be lifted up."

Psalm 76[d]

For the director of music. With stringed instruments. A psalm of Asaph. A song.

¹God is renowned in Judah;
　　in Israel his name is great.
²His tent is in Salem,
　　his dwelling place in Zion.
³There he broke the flashing arrows,
　　the shields and the swords, the weapons of war.[e]

---

[a] In Hebrew texts 75:1-10 is numbered 75:2-11.　　[b] 3 The Hebrew has *Selah* (a word of uncertain meaning) here.
[c] 4 *Horns* here symbolize strength; also in verses 5 and 10.　　[d] In Hebrew texts 76:1-12 is numbered 76:2-13.
[e] 3 The Hebrew has *Selah* (a word of uncertain meaning) here and at the end of verse 9.

⁴You are radiant with light,
      more majestic than mountains rich with game.
⁵The valiant lie plundered,
      they sleep their last sleep;
   not one of the warriors
      can lift his hands.
⁶At your rebuke, God of Jacob,
      both horse and chariot lie still.

⁷It is you alone who are to be feared.
      Who can stand before you when you are angry?
⁸From heaven you pronounced judgment,
      and the land feared and was quiet —
⁹when you, God, rose up to judge,
      to save all the afflicted of the land.
¹⁰Surely your wrath against mankind brings you praise,
      and the survivors of your wrath are restrained.ᵃ

¹¹Make vows to the Lᴏʀᴅ your God and fulfill them;
      let all the neighboring lands
      bring gifts to the One to be feared.
¹²He breaks the spirit of rulers;
      he is feared by the kings of the earth.

Psalm 77ᵇ

For the director of music. For Jeduthun. Of Asaph. A psalm.

¹I cried out to God for help;
      I cried out to God to hear me.
²When I was in distress, I sought the Lord;
      at night I stretched out untiring hands,
      and I would not be comforted.

³I remembered you, God, and I groaned;
      I meditated, and my spirit grew faint.ᶜ
⁴You kept my eyes from closing;
      I was too troubled to speak.
⁵I thought about the former days,
      the years of long ago;
⁶I remembered my songs in the night.
      My heart meditated and my spirit asked:

⁷"Will the Lord reject forever?
      Will he never show his favor again?
⁸Has his unfailing love vanished forever?
      Has his promise failed for all time?
⁹Has God forgotten to be merciful?
      Has he in anger withheld his compassion?"

ᵃ 10 Or *Surely the wrath of mankind brings you praise, / and with the remainder of wrath you arm yourself*
ᵇ In Hebrew texts 77:1-20 is numbered 77:2-21.   ᶜ 3 The Hebrew has *Selah* (a word of uncertain meaning) here
and at the end of verses 9 and 15.

10 Then I thought, "To this I will appeal:
     the years when the Most High stretched out his right hand.
11 I will remember the deeds of the LORD;
     yes, I will remember your miracles of long ago.
12 I will consider all your works
     and meditate on all your mighty deeds."

13 Your ways, God, are holy.
     What god is as great as our God?
14 You are the God who performs miracles;
     you display your power among the peoples.
15 With your mighty arm you redeemed your people,
     the descendants of Jacob and Joseph.

16 The waters saw you, God,
     the waters saw you and writhed;
     the very depths were convulsed.
17 The clouds poured down water,
     the heavens resounded with thunder;
     your arrows flashed back and forth.
18 Your thunder was heard in the whirlwind,
     your lightning lit up the world;
     the earth trembled and quaked.
19 Your path led through the sea,
     your way through the mighty waters,
     though your footprints were not seen.

20 You led your people like a flock
     by the hand of Moses and Aaron.

Psalm 78

A maskil[a] of Asaph.

1 My people, hear my teaching;
     listen to the words of my mouth.
2 I will open my mouth with a parable;
     I will utter hidden things, things from of old —
3 things we have heard and known,
     things our ancestors have told us.
4 We will not hide them from their descendants;
     we will tell the next generation
   the praiseworthy deeds of the LORD,
     his power, and the wonders he has done.
5 He decreed statutes for Jacob
     and established the law in Israel,
   which he commanded our ancestors
     to teach their children,
6 so the next generation would know them,
     even the children yet to be born,
     and they in turn would tell their children.

---

[a] Title: Probably a literary or musical term

7 Then they would put their trust in God
　　and would not forget his deeds
　　but would keep his commands.
8 They would not be like their ancestors —
　　a stubborn and rebellious generation,
　whose hearts were not loyal to God,
　　whose spirits were not faithful to him.

9 The men of Ephraim, though armed with bows,
　　turned back on the day of battle;
10 they did not keep God's covenant
　　and refused to live by his law.
11 They forgot what he had done,
　　the wonders he had shown them.
12 He did miracles in the sight of their ancestors
　　in the land of Egypt, in the region of Zoan.
13 He divided the sea and led them through;
　　he made the water stand up like a wall.
14 He guided them with the cloud by day
　　and with light from the fire all night.
15 He split the rocks in the wilderness
　　and gave them water as abundant as the seas;
16 he brought streams out of a rocky crag
　　and made water flow down like rivers.

17 But they continued to sin against him,
　　rebelling in the wilderness against the Most High.
18 They willfully put God to the test
　　by demanding the food they craved.
19 They spoke against God;
　　they said, "Can God really
　　spread a table in the wilderness?
20 True, he struck the rock,
　　and water gushed out,
　　streams flowed abundantly,
　but can he also give us bread?
　　Can he supply meat for his people?"
21 When the LORD heard them, he was furious;
　　his fire broke out against Jacob,
　　and his wrath rose against Israel,
22 for they did not believe in God
　　or trust in his deliverance.
23 Yet he gave a command to the skies above
　　and opened the doors of the heavens;
24 he rained down manna for the people to eat,
　　he gave them the grain of heaven.
25 Human beings ate the bread of angels;
　　he sent them all the food they could eat.
26 He let loose the east wind from the heavens
　　and by his power made the south wind blow.

²⁷ He rained meat down on them like dust,
 birds like sand on the seashore.
²⁸ He made them come down inside their camp,
 all around their tents.
²⁹ They ate till they were gorged —
 he had given them what they craved.
³⁰ But before they turned from what they craved,
 even while the food was still in their mouths,
³¹ God's anger rose against them;
 he put to death the sturdiest among them,
 cutting down the young men of Israel.

³² In spite of all this, they kept on sinning;
 in spite of his wonders, they did not believe.
³³ So he ended their days in futility
 and their years in terror.
³⁴ Whenever God slew them, they would seek him;
 they eagerly turned to him again.
³⁵ They remembered that God was their Rock,
 that God Most High was their Redeemer.
³⁶ But then they would flatter him with their mouths,
 lying to him with their tongues;
³⁷ their hearts were not loyal to him,
 they were not faithful to his covenant.
³⁸ Yet he was merciful;
 he forgave their iniquities
 and did not destroy them.
 Time after time he restrained his anger
 and did not stir up his full wrath.
³⁹ He remembered that they were but flesh,
 a passing breeze that does not return.

⁴⁰ How often they rebelled against him in the wilderness
 and grieved him in the wasteland!
⁴¹ Again and again they put God to the test;
 they vexed the Holy One of Israel.
⁴² They did not remember his power —
 the day he redeemed them from the oppressor,
⁴³ the day he displayed his signs in Egypt,
 his wonders in the region of Zoan.
⁴⁴ He turned their river into blood;
 they could not drink from their streams.
⁴⁵ He sent swarms of flies that devoured them,
 and frogs that devastated them.
⁴⁶ He gave their crops to the grasshopper,
 their produce to the locust.
⁴⁷ He destroyed their vines with hail
 and their sycamore-figs with sleet.
⁴⁸ He gave over their cattle to the hail,
 their livestock to bolts of lightning.

⁴⁹ He unleashed against them his hot anger,
    his wrath, indignation and hostility —
    a band of destroying angels.
⁵⁰ He prepared a path for his anger;
    he did not spare them from death
    but gave them over to the plague.
⁵¹ He struck down all the firstborn of Egypt,
    the firstfruits of manhood in the tents of Ham.
⁵² But he brought his people out like a flock;
    he led them like sheep through the wilderness.
⁵³ He guided them safely, so they were unafraid;
    but the sea engulfed their enemies.
⁵⁴ And so he brought them to the border of his holy land,
    to the hill country his right hand had taken.
⁵⁵ He drove out nations before them
    and allotted their lands to them as an inheritance;
    he settled the tribes of Israel in their homes.

⁵⁶ But they put God to the test
    and rebelled against the Most High;
    they did not keep his statutes.
⁵⁷ Like their ancestors they were disloyal and faithless,
    as unreliable as a faulty bow.
⁵⁸ They angered him with their high places;
    they aroused his jealousy with their idols.
⁵⁹ When God heard them, he was furious;
    he rejected Israel completely.
⁶⁰ He abandoned the tabernacle of Shiloh,
    the tent he had set up among humans.
⁶¹ He sent the ark of his might into captivity,
    his splendor into the hands of the enemy.
⁶² He gave his people over to the sword;
    he was furious with his inheritance.
⁶³ Fire consumed their young men,
    and their young women had no wedding songs;
⁶⁴ their priests were put to the sword,
    and their widows could not weep.

⁶⁵ Then the Lord awoke as from sleep,
    as a warrior wakes from the stupor of wine.
⁶⁶ He beat back his enemies;
    he put them to everlasting shame.
⁶⁷ Then he rejected the tents of Joseph,
    he did not choose the tribe of Ephraim;
⁶⁸ but he chose the tribe of Judah,
    Mount Zion, which he loved.
⁶⁹ He built his sanctuary like the heights,
    like the earth that he established forever.
⁷⁰ He chose David his servant
    and took him from the sheep pens;

[71] from tending the sheep he brought him
    to be the shepherd of his people Jacob,
    of Israel his inheritance.
[72] And David shepherded them with integrity of heart;
    with skillful hands he led them.

Psalm 79

A psalm of Asaph.

[1] O God, the nations have invaded your inheritance;
    they have defiled your holy temple,
    they have reduced Jerusalem to rubble.
[2] They have left the dead bodies of your servants
    as food for the birds of the sky,
    the flesh of your own people for the animals of the wild.
[3] They have poured out blood like water
    all around Jerusalem,
    and there is no one to bury the dead.
[4] We are objects of contempt to our neighbors,
    of scorn and derision to those around us.

[5] How long, Lord? Will you be angry forever?
    How long will your jealousy burn like fire?
[6] Pour out your wrath on the nations
    that do not acknowledge you,
 on the kingdoms
    that do not call on your name;
[7] for they have devoured Jacob
    and devastated his homeland.

[8] Do not hold against us the sins of past generations;
    may your mercy come quickly to meet us,
    for we are in desperate need.
[9] Help us, God our Savior,
    for the glory of your name;
 deliver us and forgive our sins
    for your name's sake.
[10] Why should the nations say,
    "Where is their God?"

 Before our eyes, make known among the nations
    that you avenge the outpoured blood of your servants.
[11] May the groans of the prisoners come before you;
    with your strong arm preserve those condemned to die.
[12] Pay back into the laps of our neighbors seven times
    the contempt they have hurled at you, Lord.
[13] Then we your people, the sheep of your pasture,
    will praise you forever;
 from generation to generation
    we will proclaim your praise.

Psalm 80[a]

For the director of music. To the tune of "The Lilies of the Covenant." Of Asaph. A psalm.

[1] Hear us, Shepherd of Israel,
    you who lead Joseph like a flock.
 You who sit enthroned between the cherubim,
    shine forth [2] before Ephraim, Benjamin and Manasseh.
 Awaken your might;
    come and save us.

[3] Restore us, O God;
    make your face shine on us,
    that we may be saved.

[4] How long, LORD God Almighty,
    will your anger smolder
    against the prayers of your people?
[5] You have fed them with the bread of tears;
    you have made them drink tears by the bowlful.
[6] You have made us an object of derision[b] to our neighbors,
    and our enemies mock us.

[7] Restore us, God Almighty;
    make your face shine on us,
    that we may be saved.

[8] You transplanted a vine from Egypt;
    you drove out the nations and planted it.
[9] You cleared the ground for it,
    and it took root and filled the land.
[10] The mountains were covered with its shade,
    the mighty cedars with its branches.
[11] Its branches reached as far as the Sea,[c]
    its shoots as far as the River.[d]

[12] Why have you broken down its walls
    so that all who pass by pick its grapes?
[13] Boars from the forest ravage it,
    and insects from the fields feed on it.
[14] Return to us, God Almighty!
    Look down from heaven and see!
 Watch over this vine,
[15]   the root your right hand has planted,
    the son[e] you have raised up for yourself.

[16] Your vine is cut down, it is burned with fire;
    at your rebuke your people perish.

---

[a] In Hebrew texts 80:1-19 is numbered 80:2-20.   [b] 6 Probable reading of the original Hebrew text; Masoretic Text contention   [c] 11 Probably the Mediterranean   [d] 11 That is, the Euphrates   [e] 15 Or branch

¹⁷Let your hand rest on the man at your right hand,
the son of man you have raised up for yourself.
¹⁸Then we will not turn away from you;
revive us, and we will call on your name.

¹⁹Restore us, LORD God Almighty;
make your face shine on us,
that we may be saved.

Psalm 81[a]

For the director of music. According to gittith.[b] Of Asaph.

¹Sing for joy to God our strength;
shout aloud to the God of Jacob!
²Begin the music, strike the timbrel,
play the melodious harp and lyre.

³Sound the ram's horn at the New Moon,
and when the moon is full, on the day of our festival;
⁴this is a decree for Israel,
an ordinance of the God of Jacob.
⁵When God went out against Egypt,
he established it as a statute for Joseph.

I heard an unknown voice say:

⁶"I removed the burden from their shoulders;
their hands were set free from the basket.
⁷In your distress you called and I rescued you,
I answered you out of a thundercloud;
I tested you at the waters of Meribah.[c]
⁸Hear me, my people, and I will warn you —
if you would only listen to me, Israel!
⁹You shall have no foreign god among you;
you shall not worship any god other than me.
¹⁰I am the LORD your God,
who brought you up out of Egypt.
Open wide your mouth and I will fill it.

¹¹"But my people would not listen to me;
Israel would not submit to me.
¹²So I gave them over to their stubborn hearts
to follow their own devices.

¹³"If my people would only listen to me,
if Israel would only follow my ways,
¹⁴how quickly I would subdue their enemies
and turn my hand against their foes!

---

a In Hebrew texts 81:1-16 is numbered 81:2-17.   *b* Title: Probably a musical term   *c* 7 The Hebrew has *Selah* (a word of uncertain meaning) here.

15 Those who hate the LORD would cringe before him,
  and their punishment would last forever.
16 But you would be fed with the finest of wheat;
  with honey from the rock I would satisfy you."

Psalm 82

A psalm of Asaph.

1 God presides in the great assembly;
  he renders judgment among the "gods":

2 "How long will you*a* defend the unjust
  and show partiality to the wicked?*b*
3 Defend the weak and the fatherless;
  uphold the cause of the poor and the oppressed.
4 Rescue the weak and the needy;
  deliver them from the hand of the wicked.

5 "The 'gods' know nothing, they understand nothing.
  They walk about in darkness;
  all the foundations of the earth are shaken.

6 "I said, 'You are "gods";
  you are all sons of the Most High.'
7 But you will die like mere mortals;
  you will fall like every other ruler."

8 Rise up, O God, judge the earth,
  for all the nations are your inheritance.

Psalm 83*c*

A song. A psalm of Asaph.

1 O God, do not remain silent;
  do not turn a deaf ear,
  do not stand aloof, O God.
2 See how your enemies growl,
  how your foes rear their heads.
3 With cunning they conspire against your people;
  they plot against those you cherish.
4 "Come," they say, "let us destroy them as a nation,
  so that Israel's name is remembered no more."

5 With one mind they plot together;
  they form an alliance against you —
6 the tents of Edom and the Ishmaelites,
  of Moab and the Hagrites,

---

a 2 The Hebrew is plural.   *b 2* The Hebrew has *Selah* (a word of uncertain meaning) here.   *c* In Hebrew texts 83:1-18 is numbered 83:2-19.

⁷Byblos, Ammon and Amalek,
　　Philistia, with the people of Tyre.
⁸Even Assyria has joined them
　　to reinforce Lot's descendants.*

⁹Do to them as you did to Midian,
　　as you did to Sisera and Jabin at the river Kishon,
¹⁰who perished at Endor
　　and became like dung on the ground.
¹¹Make their nobles like Oreb and Zeeb,
　　all their princes like Zebah and Zalmunna,
¹²who said, "Let us take possession
　　of the pasturelands of God."

¹³Make them like tumbleweed, my God,
　　like chaff before the wind.
¹⁴As fire consumes the forest
　　or a flame sets the mountains ablaze,
¹⁵so pursue them with your tempest
　　and terrify them with your storm.
¹⁶Cover their faces with shame, Lᴏʀᴅ,
　　so that they will seek your name.

¹⁷May they ever be ashamed and dismayed;
　　may they perish in disgrace.
¹⁸Let them know that you, whose name is the Lᴏʀᴅ —
　　that you alone are the Most High over all the earth.

Psalm 84*

For the director of music. According to gittith.* *Of the Sons of Korah. A psalm.*

¹How lovely is your dwelling place,
　　Lᴏʀᴅ Almighty!
²My soul yearns, even faints,
　　for the courts of the Lᴏʀᴅ;
　my heart and my flesh cry out
　　for the living God.
³Even the sparrow has found a home,
　　and the swallow a nest for herself,
　　where she may have her young —
　a place near your altar,
　　Lᴏʀᴅ Almighty, my King and my God.
⁴Blessed are those who dwell in your house;
　　they are ever praising you.*

⁵Blessed are those whose strength is in you,
　　whose hearts are set on pilgrimage.

---

a 8 The Hebrew has Selah (a word of uncertain meaning) here.　　*b* In Hebrew texts 84:1-12 is numbered 84:2-13.　　*c* Title: Probably a musical term　　*d 4* The Hebrew has Selah (a word of uncertain meaning) here and at the end of verse 8.

⁶As they pass through the Valley of Baka,
  they make it a place of springs;
  the autumn rains also cover it with pools.ᵃ
⁷They go from strength to strength,
  till each appears before God in Zion.

⁸Hear my prayer, LORD God Almighty;
  listen to me, God of Jacob.
⁹Look on our shield,ᵇ O God;
  look with favor on your anointed one.

¹⁰Better is one day in your courts
  than a thousand elsewhere;
 I would rather be a doorkeeper in the house of my God
  than dwell in the tents of the wicked.
¹¹For the LORD God is a sun and shield;
  the LORD bestows favor and honor;
 no good thing does he withhold
  from those whose walk is blameless.

¹²LORD Almighty,
  blessed is the one who trusts in you.

Psalm 85ᶜ

For the director of music. Of the Sons of Korah. A psalm.

¹You, LORD, showed favor to your land;
  you restored the fortunes of Jacob.
²You forgave the iniquity of your people
  and covered all their sins.ᵈ
³You set aside all your wrath
  and turned from your fierce anger.

⁴Restore us again, God our Savior,
  and put away your displeasure toward us.
⁵Will you be angry with us forever?
  Will you prolong your anger through all generations?
⁶Will you not revive us again,
  that your people may rejoice in you?
⁷Show us your unfailing love, LORD,
  and grant us your salvation.

⁸I will listen to what God the LORD says;
  he promises peace to his people, his faithful servants —
  but let them not turn to folly.
⁹Surely his salvation is near those who fear him,
  that his glory may dwell in our land.

ᵃ 6 Or *blessings*   ᵇ 9 Or *sovereign*   ᶜ In Hebrew texts 85:1-13 is numbered 85:2-14.   ᵈ 2 The Hebrew has *Selah* (a word of uncertain meaning) here.

¹⁰ Love and faithfulness meet together;
    righteousness and peace kiss each other.
¹¹ Faithfulness springs forth from the earth,
    and righteousness looks down from heaven.
¹² The LORD will indeed give what is good,
    and our land will yield its harvest.
¹³ Righteousness goes before him
    and prepares the way for his steps.

Psalm 86

A prayer of David.

¹ Hear me, LORD, and answer me,
    for I am poor and needy.
² Guard my life, for I am faithful to you;
    save your servant who trusts in you.
  You are my God; ³ have mercy on me, Lord,
    for I call to you all day long.
⁴ Bring joy to your servant, Lord,
    for I put my trust in you.

⁵ You, Lord, are forgiving and good,
    abounding in love to all who call to you.
⁶ Hear my prayer, LORD;
    listen to my cry for mercy.
⁷ When I am in distress, I call to you,
    because you answer me.

⁸ Among the gods there is none like you, Lord;
    no deeds can compare with yours.
⁹ All the nations you have made
    will come and worship before you, Lord;
    they will bring glory to your name.
¹⁰ For you are great and do marvelous deeds;
    you alone are God.

¹¹ Teach me your way, LORD,
    that I may rely on your faithfulness;
  give me an undivided heart,
    that I may fear your name.
¹² I will praise you, Lord my God, with all my heart;
    I will glorify your name forever.
¹³ For great is your love toward me;
    you have delivered me from the depths,
    from the realm of the dead.

¹⁴ Arrogant foes are attacking me, O God;
    ruthless people are trying to kill me —
    they have no regard for you.

15 But you, Lord, are a compassionate and gracious God,
    slow to anger, abounding in love and faithfulness.
16 Turn to me and have mercy on me;
    show your strength in behalf of your servant;
  save me, because I serve you
    just as my mother did.
17 Give me a sign of your goodness,
    that my enemies may see it and be put to shame,
    for you, Lord, have helped me and comforted me.

Psalm 87

Of the Sons of Korah. A psalm. A song.

1 He has founded his city on the holy mountain.
2 The Lord loves the gates of Zion
    more than all the other dwellings of Jacob.

3 Glorious things are said of you,
    city of God:*a*
4 "I will record Rahab*b* and Babylon
    among those who acknowledge me —
  Philistia too, and Tyre, along with Cush*c* —
    and will say, 'This one was born in Zion.' "*d*
5 Indeed, of Zion it will be said,
    "This one and that one were born in her,
    and the Most High himself will establish her."
6 The Lord will write in the register of the peoples:
    "This one was born in Zion."

7 As they make music they will sing,
    "All my fountains are in you."

Psalm 88*e*

A song. A psalm of the Sons of Korah. For the director of music. According
to mahalath leannoth.*f A maskil*g of Heman the Ezrahite.*

1 Lord, you are the God who saves me;
    day and night I cry out to you.
2 May my prayer come before you;
    turn your ear to my cry.

3 I am overwhelmed with troubles
    and my life draws near to death.
4 I am counted among those who go down to the pit;
    I am like one without strength.

---

a 3 The Hebrew has *Selah* (a word of uncertain meaning) here and at the end of verse 6.   *b 4* A poetic name
for Egypt   *c 4* That is, the upper Nile region   *d 4* Or *"I will record concerning those who acknowledge me: /*
'This one was born in Zion.' / Hear this, Rahab and Babylon, / and you too, Philistia, Tyre and Cush."   *e* In
Hebrew texts 88:1-18 is numbered 88:2-19.   *f* Title: Possibly a tune, "The Suffering of Affliction"   *g* Title:
Probably a literary or musical term

⁵I am set apart with the dead,
　　like the slain who lie in the grave,
　whom you remember no more,
　　who are cut off from your care.

⁶You have put me in the lowest pit,
　　in the darkest depths.
⁷Your wrath lies heavily on me;
　　you have overwhelmed me with all your waves.ᵃ
⁸You have taken from me my closest friends
　　and have made me repulsive to them.
　I am confined and cannot escape;
⁹　my eyes are dim with grief.

　I call to you, LORD, every day;
　　I spread out my hands to you.
¹⁰Do you show your wonders to the dead?
　　Do their spirits rise up and praise you?
¹¹Is your love declared in the grave,
　　your faithfulness in Destructionᵇ?
¹²Are your wonders known in the place of darkness,
　　or your righteous deeds in the land of oblivion?

¹³But I cry to you for help, LORD;
　　in the morning my prayer comes before you.
¹⁴Why, LORD, do you reject me
　　and hide your face from me?

¹⁵From my youth I have suffered and been close to death;
　　I have borne your terrors and am in despair.
¹⁶Your wrath has swept over me;
　　your terrors have destroyed me.
¹⁷All day long they surround me like a flood;
　　they have completely engulfed me.
¹⁸You have taken from me friend and neighbor—
　　darkness is my closest friend.

Psalm 89ᶜ

A maskilᵈ of Ethan the Ezrahite.

¹I will sing of the LORD's great love forever;
　　with my mouth I will make your faithfulness known
　　through all generations.
²I will declare that your love stands firm forever,
　　that you have established your faithfulness in heaven itself.
³You said, "I have made a covenant with my chosen one,
　　I have sworn to David my servant,
⁴'I will establish your line forever
　　and make your throne firm through all generations.'"ᵉ

ᵃ 7 The Hebrew has *Selah* (a word of uncertain meaning) here and at the end of verse 10.　　ᵇ 11 Hebrew *Abaddon*　　ᶜ In Hebrew texts 89:1-52 is numbered 89:2-53.　　ᵈ Title: Probably a literary or musical term
ᵉ 4 The Hebrew has *Selah* (a word of uncertain meaning) here and at the end of verses 37, 45 and 48.

⁵ The heavens praise your wonders, LORD,
  your faithfulness too, in the assembly of the holy ones.
⁶ For who in the skies above can compare with the LORD?
  Who is like the LORD among the heavenly beings?
⁷ In the council of the holy ones God is greatly feared;
  he is more awesome than all who surround him.
⁸ Who is like you, LORD God Almighty?
  You, LORD, are mighty, and your faithfulness surrounds you.

⁹ You rule over the surging sea;
  when its waves mount up, you still them.
¹⁰ You crushed Rahab like one of the slain;
  with your strong arm you scattered your enemies.
¹¹ The heavens are yours, and yours also the earth;
  you founded the world and all that is in it.
¹² You created the north and the south;
  Tabor and Hermon sing for joy at your name.
¹³ Your arm is endowed with power;
  your hand is strong, your right hand exalted.

¹⁴ Righteousness and justice are the foundation of your throne;
  love and faithfulness go before you.
¹⁵ Blessed are those who have learned to acclaim you,
  who walk in the light of your presence, LORD.
¹⁶ They rejoice in your name all day long;
  they celebrate your righteousness.
¹⁷ For you are their glory and strength,
  and by your favor you exalt our horn.[a]
¹⁸ Indeed, our shield[b] belongs to the LORD,
  our king to the Holy One of Israel.

¹⁹ Once you spoke in a vision,
  to your faithful people you said:
  "I have bestowed strength on a warrior;
  I have raised up a young man from among the people.
²⁰ I have found David my servant;
  with my sacred oil I have anointed him.
²¹ My hand will sustain him;
  surely my arm will strengthen him.
²² The enemy will not get the better of him;
  the wicked will not oppress him.
²³ I will crush his foes before him
  and strike down his adversaries.
²⁴ My faithful love will be with him,
  and through my name his horn[c] will be exalted.
²⁵ I will set his hand over the sea,
  his right hand over the rivers.
²⁶ He will call out to me, 'You are my Father,
  my God, the Rock my Savior.'

---

[a] 17 *Horn* here symbolizes strong one.   [b] 18 Or *sovereign*   [c] 24 *Horn* here symbolizes strength.

Life in Bible Times

What God Is Like

Psalm 89 says that God is "Lord God Almighty." He is the one who created the whole universe—the stars, the sun, the earth, and everything on it, including us. Such a powerful God is surely able to take care of us.

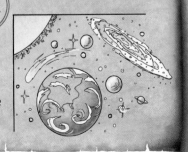

²⁷ And I will appoint him to be my firstborn,
  the most exalted of the kings of the earth.
²⁸ I will maintain my love to him forever,
  and my covenant with him will never fail.
²⁹ I will establish his line forever,
  his throne as long as the heavens endure.

³⁰ "If his sons forsake my law
  and do not follow my statutes,
³¹ if they violate my decrees
  and fail to keep my commands,
³² I will punish their sin with the rod,
  their iniquity with flogging;
³³ but I will not take my love from him,
  nor will I ever betray my faithfulness.
³⁴ I will not violate my covenant
  or alter what my lips have uttered.
³⁵ Once for all, I have sworn by my holiness —
  and I will not lie to David —
³⁶ that his line will continue forever
  and his throne endure before me like the sun;
³⁷ it will be established forever like the moon,
  the faithful witness in the sky."

³⁸ But you have rejected, you have spurned,
  you have been very angry with your anointed one.
³⁹ You have renounced the covenant with your servant
  and have defiled his crown in the dust.
⁴⁰ You have broken through all his walls
  and reduced his strongholds to ruins.
⁴¹ All who pass by have plundered him;
  he has become the scorn of his neighbors.
⁴² You have exalted the right hand of his foes;
  you have made all his enemies rejoice.
⁴³ Indeed, you have turned back the edge of his sword
  and have not supported him in battle.
⁴⁴ You have put an end to his splendor
  and cast his throne to the ground.
⁴⁵ You have cut short the days of his youth;
  you have covered him with a mantle of shame.

⁴⁶ How long, LORD? Will you hide yourself forever?
  How long will your wrath burn like fire?
⁴⁷ Remember how fleeting is my life.
  For what futility you have created all humanity!
⁴⁸ Who can live and not see death,
  or who can escape the power of the grave?
⁴⁹ Lord, where is your former great love,
  which in your faithfulness you swore to David?

⁵⁰ Remember, Lord, how your servant has*ᵃ* been mocked,
  how I bear in my heart the taunts of all the nations,
⁵¹ the taunts with which your enemies, LORD, have mocked,
  with which they have mocked every step of your anointed one.

⁵² Praise be to the LORD forever!
                    Amen and Amen.

BOOK IV

Psalms 90 – 106

Psalm 90

A prayer of Moses the man of God.

¹ Lord, you have been our dwelling place
  throughout all generations.
² Before the mountains were born
  or you brought forth the whole world,
  from everlasting to everlasting you are God.

³ You turn people back to dust,
  saying, "Return to dust, you mortals."
⁴ A thousand years in your sight
  are like a day that has just gone by,
  or like a watch in the night.
⁵ Yet you sweep people away in the sleep of death —
  they are like the new grass of the morning:
⁶ In the morning it springs up new,
  but by evening it is dry and withered.

⁷ We are consumed by your anger
  and terrified by your indignation.
⁸ You have set our iniquities before you,
  our secret sins in the light of your presence.
⁹ All our days pass away under your wrath;
  we finish our years with a moan.
¹⁰ Our days may come to seventy years,
  or eighty, if our strength endures;
  yet the best of them are but trouble and sorrow,
  for they quickly pass, and we fly away.
¹¹ If only we knew the power of your anger!
  Your wrath is as great as the fear that is your due.
¹² Teach us to number our days,
  that we may gain a heart of wisdom.

ᵃ 50 Or *your servants have*

¹³ Relent, LORD! How long will it be?
   Have compassion on your servants.
¹⁴ Satisfy us in the morning with your unfailing love,
   that we may sing for joy and be glad all our days.
¹⁵ Make us glad for as many days as you have afflicted us,
   for as many years as we have seen trouble.
¹⁶ May your deeds be shown to your servants,
   your splendor to their children.

¹⁷ May the favor[a] of the Lord our God rest on us;
   establish the work of our hands for us —
   yes, establish the work of our hands.

Psalm 91

¹ Whoever dwells in the shelter of the Most High
   will rest in the shadow of the Almighty.[b]
² I will say of the LORD, "He is my refuge and my fortress,
   my God, in whom I trust."

³ Surely he will save you
   from the fowler's snare
   and from the deadly pestilence.
⁴ He will cover you with his feathers,
   and under his wings you will find refuge;
   his faithfulness will be your shield and rampart.
⁵ You will not fear the terror of night,
   nor the arrow that flies by day,
⁶ nor the pestilence that stalks in the darkness,
   nor the plague that destroys at midday.
⁷ A thousand may fall at your side,
   ten thousand at your right hand,
   but it will not come near you.
⁸ You will only observe with your eyes
   and see the punishment of the wicked.

⁹ If you say, "The LORD is my refuge,"
   and you make the Most High your dwelling,
¹⁰ no harm will overtake you,
   no disaster will come near your tent.
¹¹ For he will command his angels concerning you
   to guard you in all your ways;
¹² they will lift you up in their hands,
   so that you will not strike your foot against a stone.
¹³ You will tread on the lion and the cobra;
   you will trample the great lion and the serpent.

¹⁴ "Because he[c] loves me," says the LORD, "I will rescue him;
   I will protect him, for he acknowledges my name.

[a] 17 Or beauty   [b] 1 Hebrew Shaddai   [c] 14 That is, probably the king

15 He will call on me, and I will answer him;
    I will be with him in trouble,
    I will deliver him and honor him.
16 With long life I will satisfy him
    and show him my salvation."

Psalm 92[a]

A psalm. A song. For the Sabbath day.

1 It is good to praise the LORD
    and make music to your name, O Most High,
2 proclaiming your love in the morning
    and your faithfulness at night,
3 to the music of the ten-stringed lyre
    and the melody of the harp.

4 For you make me glad by your deeds, LORD;
    I sing for joy at what your hands have done.
5 How great are your works, LORD,
    how profound your thoughts!
6 Senseless people do not know,
    fools do not understand,
7 that though the wicked spring up like grass
    and all evildoers flourish,
    they will be destroyed forever.

8 But you, LORD, are forever exalted.

9 For surely your enemies, LORD,
    surely your enemies will perish;
    all evildoers will be scattered.
10 You have exalted my horn[b] like that of a wild ox;
    fine oils have been poured on me.
11 My eyes have seen the defeat of my adversaries;
    my ears have heard the rout of my wicked foes.

12 The righteous will flourish like a palm tree,
    they will grow like a cedar of Lebanon;
13 planted in the house of the LORD,
    they will flourish in the courts of our God.
14 They will still bear fruit in old age,
    they will stay fresh and green,
15 proclaiming, "The LORD is upright;
    he is my Rock, and there is no wickedness in him."

Psalm 93

1 The LORD reigns, he is robed in majesty;
    the LORD is robed in majesty and armed with strength;
    indeed, the world is established, firm and secure.

---

[a] In Hebrew texts 92:1-15 is numbered 92:2-16.   [b] *10 Horn* here symbolizes strength.

2 Your throne was established long ago;
   you are from all eternity.

3 The seas have lifted up, LORD,
   the seas have lifted up their voice;
   the seas have lifted up their pounding waves.
4 Mightier than the thunder of the great waters,
   mightier than the breakers of the sea —
   the LORD on high is mighty.

5 Your statutes, LORD, stand firm;
   holiness adorns your house
   for endless days.

Psalm 94

1 The LORD is a God who avenges.
   O God who avenges, shine forth.
2 Rise up, Judge of the earth;
   pay back to the proud what they deserve.
3 How long, LORD, will the wicked,
   how long will the wicked be jubilant?

4 They pour out arrogant words;
   all the evildoers are full of boasting.
5 They crush your people, LORD;
   they oppress your inheritance.
6 They slay the widow and the foreigner;
   they murder the fatherless.
7 They say, "The LORD does not see;
   the God of Jacob takes no notice."

8 Take notice, you senseless ones among the people;
   you fools, when will you become wise?
9 Does he who fashioned the ear not hear?
   Does he who formed the eye not see?
10 Does he who disciplines nations not punish?
   Does he who teaches mankind lack knowledge?
11 The LORD knows all human plans;
   he knows that they are futile.

12 Blessed is the one you discipline, LORD,
   the one you teach from your law;
13 you grant them relief from days of trouble,
   till a pit is dug for the wicked.
14 For the LORD will not reject his people;
   he will never forsake his inheritance.
15 Judgment will again be founded on righteousness,
   and all the upright in heart will follow it.

16 Who will rise up for me against the wicked?
   Who will take a stand for me against evildoers?

17 Unless the LORD had given me help,
    I would soon have dwelt in the silence of death.
18 When I said, "My foot is slipping,"
    your unfailing love, LORD, supported me.
19 When anxiety was great within me,
    your consolation brought me joy.

20 Can a corrupt throne be allied with you —
    a throne that brings on misery by its decrees?
21 The wicked band together against the righteous
    and condemn the innocent to death.
22 But the LORD has become my fortress,
    and my God the rock in whom I take refuge.
23 He will repay them for their sins
    and destroy them for their wickedness;
    the LORD our God will destroy them.

Psalm 95

1 Come, let us sing for joy to the LORD;
    let us shout aloud to the Rock of our salvation.
2 Let us come before him with thanksgiving
    and extol him with music and song.

3 For the LORD is the great God,
    the great King above all gods.
4 In his hand are the depths of the earth,
    and the mountain peaks belong to him.
5 The sea is his, for he made it,
    and his hands formed the dry land.

6 Come, let us bow down in worship,
    let us kneel before the LORD our Maker;
7 for he is our God
    and we are the people of his pasture,
    the flock under his care.

  Today, if only you would hear his voice,
8 "Do not harden your hearts as you did at Meribah,[a]
    as you did that day at Massah[b] in the wilderness,
9 where your ancestors tested me;
    they tried me, though they had seen what I did.
10 For forty years I was angry with that generation;
    I said, 'They are a people whose hearts go astray,
    and they have not known my ways.'
11 So I declared on oath in my anger,
    'They shall never enter my rest.'"

---

a 8 Meribah means quarreling.   b 8 Massah means testing.

_____

_____

_____

_____

_____

_____

_____

_____

_____

_____

_____

_____

_____

_____

_____

_____

_____

_____

_____

Life in Bible Times

What God Is Like

Psalm 94:22 says that God is like a stronghold. A stronghold was a walled city or fortress where people went when an enemy army had invaded the land. To say that God is a stronghold means that he will keep us safe in times of danger.

Psalm 96

¹Sing to the LORD a new song;
    sing to the LORD, all the earth.
²Sing to the LORD, praise his name;
    proclaim his salvation day after day.
³Declare his glory among the nations,
    his marvelous deeds among all peoples.

⁴For great is the LORD and most worthy of praise;
    he is to be feared above all gods.
⁵For all the gods of the nations are idols,
    but the LORD made the heavens.
⁶Splendor and majesty are before him;
    strength and glory are in his sanctuary.

⁷Ascribe to the LORD, all you families of nations,
    ascribe to the LORD glory and strength.
⁸Ascribe to the LORD the glory due his name;
    bring an offering and come into his courts.
⁹Worship the LORD in the splendor of his*a* holiness;
    tremble before him, all the earth.
¹⁰Say among the nations, "The LORD reigns."
    The world is firmly established, it cannot be moved;
    he will judge the peoples with equity.

¹¹Let the heavens rejoice, let the earth be glad;
    let the sea resound, and all that is in it.
¹²Let the fields be jubilant, and everything in them;
    let all the trees of the forest sing for joy.
¹³Let all creation rejoice before the LORD, for he comes,
    he comes to judge the earth.
  He will judge the world in righteousness
    and the peoples in his faithfulness.

Psalm 97

¹The LORD reigns, let the earth be glad;
    let the distant shores rejoice.
²Clouds and thick darkness surround him;
    righteousness and justice are the foundation of his throne.
³Fire goes before him
    and consumes his foes on every side.
⁴His lightning lights up the world;
    the earth sees and trembles.
⁵The mountains melt like wax before the LORD,
    before the Lord of all the earth.
⁶The heavens proclaim his righteousness,
    and all peoples see his glory.

a 9 Or LORD *with the splendor of*

7 All who worship images are put to shame,
   those who boast in idols —
   worship him, all you gods!

8 Zion hears and rejoices
   and the villages of Judah are glad
   because of your judgments, LORD.
9 For you, LORD, are the Most High over all the earth;
   you are exalted far above all gods.
10 Let those who love the LORD hate evil,
   for he guards the lives of his faithful ones
   and delivers them from the hand of the wicked.
11 Light shines[a] on the righteous
   and joy on the upright in heart.
12 Rejoice in the LORD, you who are righteous,
   and praise his holy name.

Psalm 98

A psalm.

1 Sing to the LORD a new song,
   for he has done marvelous things;
 his right hand and his holy arm
   have worked salvation for him.
2 The LORD has made his salvation known
   and revealed his righteousness to the nations.
3 He has remembered his love
   and his faithfulness to Israel;
 all the ends of the earth have seen
   the salvation of our God.

4 Shout for joy to the LORD, all the earth,
   burst into jubilant song with music;
5 make music to the LORD with the harp,
   with the harp and the sound of singing,
6 with trumpets and the blast of the ram's horn —
   shout for joy before the LORD, the King.

7 Let the sea resound, and everything in it,
   the world, and all who live in it.
8 Let the rivers clap their hands,
   let the mountains sing together for joy;
9 let them sing before the LORD,
   for he comes to judge the earth.
 He will judge the world in righteousness
   and the peoples with equity.

---

a 11 One Hebrew manuscript and ancient versions (see also 112:4); most Hebrew manuscripts *Light is sown*

Psalm 99

[1] The LORD reigns,
    let the nations tremble;
 he sits enthroned between the cherubim,
    let the earth shake.
[2] Great is the LORD in Zion;
    he is exalted over all the nations.
[3] Let them praise your great and awesome name —
    he is holy.

[4] The King is mighty, he loves justice —
    you have established equity;
 in Jacob you have done
    what is just and right.
[5] Exalt the LORD our God
    and worship at his footstool;
    he is holy.

[6] Moses and Aaron were among his priests,
    Samuel was among those who called on his name;
 they called on the LORD
    and he answered them.
[7] He spoke to them from the pillar of cloud;
    they kept his statutes and the decrees he gave them.

[8] LORD our God,
    you answered them;
 you were to Israel a forgiving God,
    though you punished their misdeeds.[a]
[9] Exalt the LORD our God
    and worship at his holy mountain,
    for the LORD our God is holy.

Psalm 100

A psalm. For giving grateful praise.

[1] Shout for joy to the LORD, all the earth.
[2]   Worship the LORD with gladness;
    come before him with joyful songs.
[3] Know that the LORD is God.
    It is he who made us, and we are his[b];
    we are his people, the sheep of his pasture.

[4] Enter his gates with thanksgiving
    and his courts with praise;
    give thanks to him and praise his name.
[5] For the LORD is good and his love endures forever;
    his faithfulness continues through all generations.

---

a 8 Or *God, / an avenger of the wrongs done to them*   *b 3* Or *and not we ourselves*

Psalm 101

Of David. A psalm.

1 I will sing of your love and justice;
    to you, LORD, I will sing praise.
2 I will be careful to lead a blameless life —
    when will you come to me?

  I will conduct the affairs of my house
    with a blameless heart.
3 I will not look with approval
    on anything that is vile.

  I hate what faithless people do;
    I will have no part in it.
4 The perverse of heart shall be far from me;
    I will have nothing to do with what is evil.

5 Whoever slanders their neighbor in secret,
    I will put to silence;
  whoever has haughty eyes and a proud heart,
    I will not tolerate.

6 My eyes will be on the faithful in the land,
    that they may dwell with me;
  the one whose walk is blameless
    will minister to me.

7 No one who practices deceit
    will dwell in my house;
  no one who speaks falsely
    will stand in my presence.

8 Every morning I will put to silence
    all the wicked in the land;
  I will cut off every evildoer
    from the city of the LORD.

Psalm 102[a]

*A prayer of an afflicted person who has grown weak
and pours out a lament before the LORD.*

1 Hear my prayer, LORD;
    let my cry for help come to you.
2 Do not hide your face from me
    when I am in distress.
  Turn your ear to me;
    when I call, answer me quickly.

[a] In Hebrew texts 102:1-28 is numbered 102:2-29.

³ For my days vanish like smoke;
    my bones burn like glowing embers.
⁴ My heart is blighted and withered like grass;
    I forget to eat my food.
⁵ In my distress I groan aloud
    and am reduced to skin and bones.
⁶ I am like a desert owl,
    like an owl among the ruins.
⁷ I lie awake; I have become
    like a bird alone on a roof.
⁸ All day long my enemies taunt me;
    those who rail against me use my name as a curse.
⁹ For I eat ashes as my food
    and mingle my drink with tears
¹⁰ because of your great wrath,
    for you have taken me up and thrown me aside.
¹¹ My days are like the evening shadow;
    I wither away like grass.

¹² But you, LORD, sit enthroned forever;
    your renown endures through all generations.
¹³ You will arise and have compassion on Zion,
    for it is time to show favor to her;
    the appointed time has come.
¹⁴ For her stones are dear to your servants;
    her very dust moves them to pity.
¹⁵ The nations will fear the name of the LORD,
    all the kings of the earth will revere your glory.
¹⁶ For the LORD will rebuild Zion
    and appear in his glory.
¹⁷ He will respond to the prayer of the destitute;
    he will not despise their plea.

¹⁸ Let this be written for a future generation,
    that a people not yet created may praise the LORD:
¹⁹ "The LORD looked down from his sanctuary on high,
    from heaven he viewed the earth,
²⁰ to hear the groans of the prisoners
    and release those condemned to death."
²¹ So the name of the LORD will be declared in Zion
    and his praise in Jerusalem
²² when the peoples and the kingdoms
    assemble to worship the LORD.

²³ In the course of my life[a] he broke my strength;
    he cut short my days.
²⁴ So I said:
  "Do not take me away, my God, in the midst of my days;
    your years go on through all generations.

[a] 23 Or *By his power*

Tell God Your Feelings

No one likes to feel upset. Or afraid. Or angry. But sometimes we all have feelings like these. Read the first 11 verses of Psalm 102. In the space below, write what words tell you how the psalmist felt.

The person who wrote this psalm knew that God would listen to his feelings and that telling God would help. Next time you're feeling bad, write down your feelings for God to see. Maybe by the time you're finished writing you'll already feel better, just like the person who wrote this psalm (see Psalm 102:16–17).

Psalm 102:1–11

_____

_____

_____

_____

_____

_____

_____

_____

_____

_____

_____

_____

_____

_____

_____

_____

_____

_____

_____

25 In the beginning you laid the foundations of the earth,
and the heavens are the work of your hands.
26 They will perish, but you remain;
they will all wear out like a garment.
Like clothing you will change them
and they will be discarded.
27 But you remain the same,
and your years will never end.
28 The children of your servants will live in your presence;
their descendants will be established before you."

Psalm 103

Of David.

1 Praise the LORD, my soul;
all my inmost being, praise his holy name.
2 Praise the LORD, my soul,
and forget not all his benefits —
3 who forgives all your sins
and heals all your diseases,
4 who redeems your life from the pit
and crowns you with love and compassion,
5 who satisfies your desires with good things
so that your youth is renewed like the eagle's.

6 The LORD works righteousness
and justice for all the oppressed.

7 He made known his ways to Moses,
his deeds to the people of Israel:
8 The LORD is compassionate and gracious,
slow to anger, abounding in love.
9 He will not always accuse,
nor will he harbor his anger forever;
10 he does not treat us as our sins deserve
or repay us according to our iniquities.
11 For as high as the heavens are above the earth,
so great is his love for those who fear him;
12 as far as the east is from the west,
so far has he removed our transgressions from us.

13 As a father has compassion on his children,
so the LORD has compassion on those who fear him;
14 for he knows how we are formed,
he remembers that we are dust.
15 The life of mortals is like grass,
they flourish like a flower of the field;
16 the wind blows over it and it is gone,
and its place remembers it no more.

_____

_____

_____

_____

_____

_____

_____

_____

_____

_____

_____

_____

_____

_____

_____

_____

_____

_____

_____

_____

_____

Life in Bible Times

What God Is Like

Psalm 103:13 says that God is like a compassionate father. This means that God loves us very much. He made us, and he knows us better than we know ourselves. He will not stay angry when we sin, but he will forgive us.

17 But from everlasting to everlasting
    the LORD's love is with those who fear him,
    and his righteousness with their children's children —
18 with those who keep his covenant
    and remember to obey his precepts.

19 The LORD has established his throne in heaven,
    and his kingdom rules over all.

20 Praise the LORD, you his angels,
    you mighty ones who do his bidding,
    who obey his word.
21 Praise the LORD, all his heavenly hosts,
    you his servants who do his will.
22 Praise the LORD, all his works
    everywhere in his dominion.

    Praise the LORD, my soul.

Psalm 104

1 Praise the LORD, my soul.

LORD my God, you are very great;
    you are clothed with splendor and majesty.

2 The LORD wraps himself in light as with a garment;
    he stretches out the heavens like a tent
3   and lays the beams of his upper chambers on their waters.
He makes the clouds his chariot
    and rides on the wings of the wind.
4 He makes winds his messengers,*a*
    flames of fire his servants.

5 He set the earth on its foundations;
    it can never be moved.
6 You covered it with the watery depths as with a garment;
    the waters stood above the mountains.
7 But at your rebuke the waters fled,
    at the sound of your thunder they took to flight;
8 they flowed over the mountains,
    they went down into the valleys,
    to the place you assigned for them.
9 You set a boundary they cannot cross;
    never again will they cover the earth.

10 He makes springs pour water into the ravines;
    it flows between the mountains.
11 They give water to all the beasts of the field;
    the wild donkeys quench their thirst.
12 The birds of the sky nest by the waters;
    they sing among the branches.

a 4 Or angels

¹³ He waters the mountains from his upper chambers;
    the land is satisfied by the fruit of his work.
¹⁴ He makes grass grow for the cattle,
    and plants for people to cultivate —
    bringing forth food from the earth:
¹⁵ wine that gladdens human hearts,
    oil to make their faces shine,
    and bread that sustains their hearts.
¹⁶ The trees of the LORD are well watered,
    the cedars of Lebanon that he planted.
¹⁷ There the birds make their nests;
    the stork has its home in the junipers.
¹⁸ The high mountains belong to the wild goats;
    the crags are a refuge for the hyrax.

¹⁹ He made the moon to mark the seasons,
    and the sun knows when to go down.
²⁰ You bring darkness, it becomes night,
    and all the beasts of the forest prowl.
²¹ The lions roar for their prey
    and seek their food from God.
²² The sun rises, and they steal away;
    they return and lie down in their dens.
²³ Then people go out to their work,
    to their labor until evening.

²⁴ How many are your works, LORD!
    In wisdom you made them all;
    the earth is full of your creatures.
²⁵ There is the sea, vast and spacious,
    teeming with creatures beyond number —
    living things both large and small.
²⁶ There the ships go to and fro,
    and Leviathan, which you formed to frolic there.

²⁷ All creatures look to you
    to give them their food at the proper time.
²⁸ When you give it to them,
    they gather it up;
  when you open your hand,
    they are satisfied with good things.
²⁹ When you hide your face,
    they are terrified;
  when you take away their breath,
    they die and return to the dust.
³⁰ When you send your Spirit,
    they are created,
    and you renew the face of the ground.

³¹May the glory of the LORD endure forever;
    may the LORD rejoice in his works —
³²he who looks at the earth, and it trembles,
    who touches the mountains, and they smoke.

³³I will sing to the LORD all my life;
    I will sing praise to my God as long as I live.
³⁴May my meditation be pleasing to him,
    as I rejoice in the LORD.
³⁵But may sinners vanish from the earth
    and the wicked be no more.

Praise the LORD, my soul.

Praise the LORD.^a

Psalm 105

¹Give praise to the LORD, proclaim his name;
    make known among the nations what he has done.
²Sing to him, sing praise to him;
    tell of all his wonderful acts.
³Glory in his holy name;
    let the hearts of those who seek the LORD rejoice.
⁴Look to the LORD and his strength;
    seek his face always.

⁵Remember the wonders he has done,
    his miracles, and the judgments he pronounced,
⁶you his servants, the descendants of Abraham,
    his chosen ones, the children of Jacob.
⁷He is the LORD our God;
    his judgments are in all the earth.

⁸He remembers his covenant forever,
    the promise he made, for a thousand generations,
⁹the covenant he made with Abraham,
    the oath he swore to Isaac.
¹⁰He confirmed it to Jacob as a decree,
    to Israel as an everlasting covenant:
¹¹"To you I will give the land of Canaan
    as the portion you will inherit."

¹²When they were but few in number,
    few indeed, and strangers in it,
¹³they wandered from nation to nation,
    from one kingdom to another.
¹⁴He allowed no one to oppress them;
    for their sake he rebuked kings:
¹⁵"Do not touch my anointed ones;
    do my prophets no harm."

^a 35 Hebrew *Hallelu Yah*; in the Septuagint this line stands at the beginning of Psalm 105.

16 He called down famine on the land
    and destroyed all their supplies of food;
17 and he sent a man before them —
    Joseph, sold as a slave.
18 They bruised his feet with shackles,
    his neck was put in irons,
19 till what he foretold came to pass,
    till the word of the LORD proved him true.
20 The king sent and released him,
    the ruler of peoples set him free.
21 He made him master of his household,
    ruler over all he possessed,
22 to instruct his princes as he pleased
    and teach his elders wisdom.

23 Then Israel entered Egypt;
    Jacob resided as a foreigner in the land of Ham.
24 The LORD made his people very fruitful;
    he made them too numerous for their foes,
25 whose hearts he turned to hate his people,
    to conspire against his servants.
26 He sent Moses his servant,
    and Aaron, whom he had chosen.
27 They performed his signs among them,
    his wonders in the land of Ham.
28 He sent darkness and made the land dark —
    for had they not rebelled against his words?
29 He turned their waters into blood,
    causing their fish to die.
30 Their land teemed with frogs,
    which went up into the bedrooms of their rulers.
31 He spoke, and there came swarms of flies,
    and gnats throughout their country.
32 He turned their rain into hail,
    with lightning throughout their land;
33 he struck down their vines and fig trees
    and shattered the trees of their country.
34 He spoke, and the locusts came,
    grasshoppers without number;
35 they ate up every green thing in their land,
    ate up the produce of their soil.
36 Then he struck down all the firstborn in their land,
    the firstfruits of all their manhood.
37 He brought out Israel, laden with silver and gold,
    and from among their tribes no one faltered.
38 Egypt was glad when they left,
    because dread of Israel had fallen on them.

39 He spread out a cloud as a covering,
    and a fire to give light at night.

⁴⁰ They asked, and he brought them quail;
   he fed them well with the bread of heaven.
⁴¹ He opened the rock, and water gushed out;
   it flowed like a river in the desert.

⁴² For he remembered his holy promise
   given to his servant Abraham.
⁴³ He brought out his people with rejoicing,
   his chosen ones with shouts of joy;
⁴⁴ he gave them the lands of the nations,
   and they fell heir to what others had toiled for —
⁴⁵ that they might keep his precepts
   and observe his laws.

Praise the Lord.ᵃ

Psalm 106

¹ Praise the Lord.ᵇ

Give thanks to the Lord, for he is good;
   his love endures forever.

² Who can proclaim the mighty acts of the Lord
   or fully declare his praise?
³ Blessed are those who act justly,
   who always do what is right.

⁴ Remember me, Lord, when you show favor to your people,
   come to my aid when you save them,
⁵ that I may enjoy the prosperity of your chosen ones,
   that I may share in the joy of your nation
   and join your inheritance in giving praise.

⁶ We have sinned, even as our ancestors did;
   we have done wrong and acted wickedly.
⁷ When our ancestors were in Egypt,
   they gave no thought to your miracles;
   they did not remember your many kindnesses,
   and they rebelled by the sea, the Red Sea.ᶜ
⁸ Yet he saved them for his name's sake,
   to make his mighty power known.
⁹ He rebuked the Red Sea, and it dried up;
   he led them through the depths as through a desert.
¹⁰ He saved them from the hand of the foe;
   from the hand of the enemy he redeemed them.
¹¹ The waters covered their adversaries;
   not one of them survived.
¹² Then they believed his promises
   and sang his praise.

ᵃ 45 Hebrew *Hallelu Yah*   ᵇ 1 Hebrew *Hallelu Yah*; also in verse 48   ᶜ 7 Or *the Sea of Reeds*; also in verses 9 and 22

¹³ But they soon forgot what he had done
    and did not wait for his plan to unfold.
¹⁴ In the desert they gave in to their craving;
    in the wilderness they put God to the test.
¹⁵ So he gave them what they asked for,
    but sent a wasting disease among them.

¹⁶ In the camp they grew envious of Moses
    and of Aaron, who was consecrated to the LORD.
¹⁷ The earth opened up and swallowed Dathan;
    it buried the company of Abiram.
¹⁸ Fire blazed among their followers;
    a flame consumed the wicked.
¹⁹ At Horeb they made a calf
    and worshiped an idol cast from metal.
²⁰ They exchanged their glorious God
    for an image of a bull, which eats grass.
²¹ They forgot the God who saved them,
    who had done great things in Egypt,
²² miracles in the land of Ham
    and awesome deeds by the Red Sea.
²³ So he said he would destroy them —
    had not Moses, his chosen one,
  stood in the breach before him
    to keep his wrath from destroying them.

²⁴ Then they despised the pleasant land;
    they did not believe his promise.
²⁵ They grumbled in their tents
    and did not obey the LORD.
²⁶ So he swore to them with uplifted hand
    that he would make them fall in the wilderness,
²⁷ make their descendants fall among the nations
    and scatter them throughout the lands.

²⁸ They yoked themselves to the Baal of Peor
    and ate sacrifices offered to lifeless gods;
²⁹ they aroused the LORD's anger by their wicked deeds,
    and a plague broke out among them.
³⁰ But Phinehas stood up and intervened,
    and the plague was checked.
³¹ This was credited to him as righteousness
    for endless generations to come.
³² By the waters of Meribah they angered the LORD,
    and trouble came to Moses because of them;
³³ for they rebelled against the Spirit of God,
    and rash words came from Moses' lips.ᵃ

ᵃ 33 Or *against his spirit, / and rash words came from his lips*

³⁴ They did not destroy the peoples
as the Lord had commanded them,
³⁵ but they mingled with the nations
and adopted their customs.
³⁶ They worshiped their idols,
which became a snare to them.
³⁷ They sacrificed their sons
and their daughters to false gods.
³⁸ They shed innocent blood,
the blood of their sons and daughters,
whom they sacrificed to the idols of Canaan,
and the land was desecrated by their blood.
³⁹ They defiled themselves by what they did;
by their deeds they prostituted themselves.

⁴⁰ Therefore the Lord was angry with his people
and abhorred his inheritance.
⁴¹ He gave them into the hands of the nations,
and their foes ruled over them.
⁴² Their enemies oppressed them
and subjected them to their power.
⁴³ Many times he delivered them,
but they were bent on rebellion
and they wasted away in their sin.
⁴⁴ Yet he took note of their distress
when he heard their cry;
⁴⁵ for their sake he remembered his covenant
and out of his great love he relented.
⁴⁶ He caused all who held them captive
to show them mercy.

⁴⁷ Save us, Lord our God,
and gather us from the nations,
that we may give thanks to your holy name
and glory in your praise.

⁴⁸ Praise be to the Lord, the God of Israel,
from everlasting to everlasting.

Let all the people say, "Amen!"

Praise the Lord.

BOOK V

Psalms 107 – 150

Psalm 107

¹Give thanks to the Lord, for he is good;
    his love endures forever.

²Let the redeemed of the Lord tell their story —
    those he redeemed from the hand of the foe,
³those he gathered from the lands,
    from east and west, from north and south.*ᵃ*

⁴Some wandered in desert wastelands,
    finding no way to a city where they could settle.
⁵They were hungry and thirsty,
    and their lives ebbed away.
⁶Then they cried out to the Lord in their trouble,
    and he delivered them from their distress.
⁷He led them by a straight way
    to a city where they could settle.
⁸Let them give thanks to the Lord for his unfailing love
    and his wonderful deeds for mankind,
⁹for he satisfies the thirsty
    and fills the hungry with good things.

¹⁰Some sat in darkness, in utter darkness,
    prisoners suffering in iron chains,
¹¹because they rebelled against God's commands
    and despised the plans of the Most High.
¹²So he subjected them to bitter labor;
    they stumbled, and there was no one to help.
¹³Then they cried to the Lord in their trouble,
    and he saved them from their distress.
¹⁴He brought them out of darkness, the utter darkness,
    and broke away their chains.
¹⁵Let them give thanks to the Lord for his unfailing love
    and his wonderful deeds for mankind,
¹⁶for he breaks down gates of bronze
    and cuts through bars of iron.

¹⁷Some became fools through their rebellious ways
    and suffered affliction because of their iniquities.
¹⁸They loathed all food
    and drew near the gates of death.
¹⁹Then they cried to the Lord in their trouble,
    and he saved them from their distress.
²⁰He sent out his word and healed them;
    he rescued them from the grave.

ᵃ 3 Hebrew north and the sea

²¹ Let them give thanks to the Lord for his unfailing love
  and his wonderful deeds for mankind.
²² Let them sacrifice thank offerings
  and tell of his works with songs of joy.

²³ Some went out on the sea in ships;
  they were merchants on the mighty waters.
²⁴ They saw the works of the Lord,
  his wonderful deeds in the deep.
²⁵ For he spoke and stirred up a tempest
  that lifted high the waves.
²⁶ They mounted up to the heavens and went down to the depths;
  in their peril their courage melted away.
²⁷ They reeled and staggered like drunkards;
  they were at their wits' end.
²⁸ Then they cried out to the Lord in their trouble,
  and he brought them out of their distress.
²⁹ He stilled the storm to a whisper;
  the waves of the sea*ᵃ* were hushed.
³⁰ They were glad when it grew calm,
  and he guided them to their desired haven.
³¹ Let them give thanks to the Lord for his unfailing love
  and his wonderful deeds for mankind.
³² Let them exalt him in the assembly of the people
  and praise him in the council of the elders.

³³ He turned rivers into a desert,
  flowing springs into thirsty ground,
³⁴ and fruitful land into a salt waste,
  because of the wickedness of those who lived there.
³⁵ He turned the desert into pools of water
  and the parched ground into flowing springs;
³⁶ there he brought the hungry to live,
  and they founded a city where they could settle.
³⁷ They sowed fields and planted vineyards
  that yielded a fruitful harvest;
³⁸ he blessed them, and their numbers greatly increased,
  and he did not let their herds diminish.

³⁹ Then their numbers decreased, and they were humbled
  by oppression, calamity and sorrow;
⁴⁰ he who pours contempt on nobles
  made them wander in a trackless waste.
⁴¹ But he lifted the needy out of their affliction
  and increased their families like flocks.
⁴² The upright see and rejoice,
  but all the wicked shut their mouths.

⁴³ Let the one who is wise heed these things
  and ponder the loving deeds of the Lord.

ᵃ 29 Dead Sea Scrolls; Masoretic Text / *their waves*

Psalm 108[a]

A song. A psalm of David.

[1] My heart, O God, is steadfast;
　　I will sing and make music with all my soul.
[2] Awake, harp and lyre!
　　I will awaken the dawn.
[3] I will praise you, LORD, among the nations;
　　I will sing of you among the peoples.
[4] For great is your love, higher than the heavens;
　　your faithfulness reaches to the skies.
[5] Be exalted, O God, above the heavens;
　　let your glory be over all the earth.

[6] Save us and help us with your right hand,
　　that those you love may be delivered.
[7] God has spoken from his sanctuary:
　　"In triumph I will parcel out Shechem
　　and measure off the Valley of Sukkoth.
[8] Gilead is mine, Manasseh is mine;
　　Ephraim is my helmet,
　　Judah is my scepter.
[9] Moab is my washbasin,
　　on Edom I toss my sandal;
　　over Philistia I shout in triumph."

[10] Who will bring me to the fortified city?
　　Who will lead me to Edom?
[11] Is it not you, God, you who have rejected us
　　and no longer go out with our armies?
[12] Give us aid against the enemy,
　　for human help is worthless.
[13] With God we will gain the victory,
　　and he will trample down our enemies.

Psalm 109

For the director of music. Of David. A psalm.

[1] My God, whom I praise,
　　do not remain silent,
[2] for people who are wicked and deceitful
　　have opened their mouths against me;
　　they have spoken against me with lying tongues.
[3] With words of hatred they surround me;
　　they attack me without cause.
[4] In return for my friendship they accuse me,
　　but I am a man of prayer.
[5] They repay me evil for good,
　　and hatred for my friendship.

[a] In Hebrew texts 108:1-13 is numbered 108:2-14.

⁶Appoint someone evil to oppose my enemy;
    let an accuser stand at his right hand.
⁷When he is tried, let him be found guilty,
    and may his prayers condemn him.
⁸May his days be few;
    may another take his place of leadership.
⁹May his children be fatherless
    and his wife a widow.
¹⁰May his children be wandering beggars;
    may they be driven[a] from their ruined homes.
¹¹May a creditor seize all he has;
    may strangers plunder the fruits of his labor.
¹²May no one extend kindness to him
    or take pity on his fatherless children.
¹³May his descendants be cut off,
    their names blotted out from the next generation.
¹⁴May the iniquity of his fathers be remembered before the LORD;
    may the sin of his mother never be blotted out.
¹⁵May their sins always remain before the LORD,
    that he may blot out their name from the earth.

¹⁶For he never thought of doing a kindness,
    but hounded to death the poor
    and the needy and the brokenhearted.
¹⁷He loved to pronounce a curse —
    may it come back on him.
  He found no pleasure in blessing —
    may it be far from him.
¹⁸He wore cursing as his garment;
    it entered into his body like water,
    into his bones like oil.
¹⁹May it be like a cloak wrapped about him,
    like a belt tied forever around him.
²⁰May this be the LORD's payment to my accusers,
    to those who speak evil of me.

²¹But you, Sovereign LORD,
    help me for your name's sake;
    out of the goodness of your love, deliver me.
²²For I am poor and needy,
    and my heart is wounded within me.
²³I fade away like an evening shadow;
    I am shaken off like a locust.
²⁴My knees give way from fasting;
    my body is thin and gaunt.
²⁵I am an object of scorn to my accusers;
    when they see me, they shake their heads.

---

[a] 10 Septuagint; Hebrew sought

26 Help me, LORD my God;
    save me according to your unfailing love.
27 Let them know that it is your hand,
    that you, LORD, have done it.
28 While they curse, may you bless;
    may those who attack me be put to shame,
    but may your servant rejoice.
29 May my accusers be clothed with disgrace
    and wrapped in shame as in a cloak.

30 With my mouth I will greatly extol the LORD;
    in the great throng of worshipers I will praise him.
31 For he stands at the right hand of the needy,
    to save their lives from those who would condemn them.

Psalm 110

Of David. A psalm.

1 The LORD says to my lord:[a]

"Sit at my right hand
    until I make your enemies
    a footstool for your feet."

2 The LORD will extend your mighty scepter from Zion, saying,
    "Rule in the midst of your enemies!"
3 Your troops will be willing
    on your day of battle.
Arrayed in holy splendor,
    your young men will come to you
    like dew from the morning's womb.[b]

4 The LORD has sworn
    and will not change his mind:
    "You are a priest forever,
    in the order of Melchizedek."

5 The Lord is at your right hand[c];
    he will crush kings on the day of his wrath.
6 He will judge the nations, heaping up the dead
    and crushing the rulers of the whole earth.
7 He will drink from a brook along the way,[d]
    and so he will lift his head high.

Psalm 111[e]

1 Praise the LORD.[f]

I will extol the LORD with all my heart
    in the council of the upright and in the assembly.

---

[a] 1 Or *Lord*   [b] 3 The meaning of the Hebrew for this sentence is uncertain.   [c] 5 Or *My lord is at your right hand, LORD*   [d] 7 The meaning of the Hebrew for this clause is uncertain.   [e] This psalm is an acrostic poem, the lines of which begin with the successive letters of the Hebrew alphabet.   [f] 1 Hebrew *Hallelu Yah*

² Great are the works of the Lord;
  they are pondered by all who delight in them.
³ Glorious and majestic are his deeds,
  and his righteousness endures forever.
⁴ He has caused his wonders to be remembered;
  the Lord is gracious and compassionate.
⁵ He provides food for those who fear him;
  he remembers his covenant forever.

⁶ He has shown his people the power of his works,
  giving them the lands of other nations.
⁷ The works of his hands are faithful and just;
  all his precepts are trustworthy.
⁸ They are established for ever and ever,
  enacted in faithfulness and uprightness.
⁹ He provided redemption for his people;
  he ordained his covenant forever —
  holy and awesome is his name.

¹⁰ The fear of the Lord is the beginning of wisdom;
  all who follow his precepts have good understanding.
  To him belongs eternal praise.

Psalm 112ᵃ

¹ Praise the Lord.ᵇ

 Blessed are those who fear the Lord,
  who find great delight in his commands.

² Their children will be mighty in the land;
  the generation of the upright will be blessed.
³ Wealth and riches are in their houses,
  and their righteousness endures forever.
⁴ Even in darkness light dawns for the upright,
  for those who are gracious and compassionate and righteous.
⁵ Good will come to those who are generous and lend freely,
  who conduct their affairs with justice.

⁶ Surely the righteous will never be shaken;
  they will be remembered forever.
⁷ They will have no fear of bad news;
  their hearts are steadfast, trusting in the Lord.
⁸ Their hearts are secure, they will have no fear;
  in the end they will look in triumph on their foes.
⁹ They have freely scattered their gifts to the poor,
  their righteousness endures forever;
  their hornᶜ will be lifted high in honor.

¹⁰ The wicked will see and be vexed,
  they will gnash their teeth and waste away;
  the longings of the wicked will come to nothing.

ᵃ This psalm is an acrostic poem, the lines of which begin with the successive letters of the Hebrew alphabet.
ᵇ 1 Hebrew *Hallelu Yah*   ᶜ 9 *Horn* here symbolizes dignity.

Psalm 113

[1] Praise the LORD.[a]

Praise the LORD, you his servants;
    praise the name of the LORD.
[2] Let the name of the LORD be praised,
    both now and forevermore.
[3] From the rising of the sun to the place where it sets,
    the name of the LORD is to be praised.

[4] The LORD is exalted over all the nations,
    his glory above the heavens.
[5] Who is like the LORD our God,
    the One who sits enthroned on high,
[6] who stoops down to look
    on the heavens and the earth?

[7] He raises the poor from the dust
    and lifts the needy from the ash heap;
[8] he seats them with princes,
    with the princes of his people.
[9] He settles the childless woman in her home
    as a happy mother of children.

Praise the LORD.

Psalm 114

[1] When Israel came out of Egypt,
    Jacob from a people of foreign tongue,
[2] Judah became God's sanctuary,
    Israel his dominion.

[3] The sea looked and fled,
    the Jordan turned back;
[4] the mountains leaped like rams,
    the hills like lambs.

[5] Why was it, sea, that you fled?
    Why, Jordan, did you turn back?
[6] Why, mountains, did you leap like rams,
    you hills, like lambs?

[7] Tremble, earth, at the presence of the Lord,
    at the presence of the God of Jacob,
[8] who turned the rock into a pool,
    the hard rock into springs of water.

---

[a] 1 Hebrew *Hallelu Yah*; also in verse 9

Praise God

Praise is telling God how great he is. Sometimes we praise God by talking to him. Sometimes we praise God by talking to others about him. Read Psalm 113.

You can praise God too. Write down two lines telling God what you like about him. Then, write down two lines that tell others why God is so special. When it's your turn to pray before a meal or when you pray at bedtime, start with one of the praise verses you have written.

Psalm 113:1-9

_____

_____

_____

_____

_____

_____

_____

_____

_____

_____

_____

_____

_____

_____

_____

_____

_____

_____

Psalm 115

¹Not to us, LORD, not to us
 but to your name be the glory,
  because of your love and faithfulness.

²Why do the nations say,
 "Where is their God?"
³Our God is in heaven;
 he does whatever pleases him.
⁴But their idols are silver and gold,
 made by human hands.
⁵They have mouths, but cannot speak,
 eyes, but cannot see.
⁶They have ears, but cannot hear,
 noses, but cannot smell.
⁷They have hands, but cannot feel,
 feet, but cannot walk,
  nor can they utter a sound with their throats.
⁸Those who make them will be like them,
 and so will all who trust in them.

⁹All you Israelites, trust in the LORD —
 he is their help and shield.
¹⁰House of Aaron, trust in the LORD —
 he is their help and shield.
¹¹You who fear him, trust in the LORD —
 he is their help and shield.

¹²The LORD remembers us and will bless us:
 He will bless his people Israel,
 he will bless the house of Aaron,
¹³he will bless those who fear the LORD —
 small and great alike.

¹⁴May the LORD cause you to flourish,
 both you and your children.
¹⁵May you be blessed by the LORD,
 the Maker of heaven and earth.

¹⁶The highest heavens belong to the LORD,
 but the earth he has given to mankind.
¹⁷It is not the dead who praise the LORD,
 those who go down to the place of silence;
¹⁸it is we who extol the LORD,
 both now and forevermore.

Praise the LORD.ᵃ

ᵃ 18 Hebrew *Hallelu Yah*

Psalm 116

1 I love the LORD, for he heard my voice;
 he heard my cry for mercy.
2 Because he turned his ear to me,
 I will call on him as long as I live.

3 The cords of death entangled me,
 the anguish of the grave came over me;
 I was overcome by distress and sorrow.
4 Then I called on the name of the LORD:
 "LORD, save me!"

5 The LORD is gracious and righteous;
 our God is full of compassion.
6 The LORD protects the unwary;
 when I was brought low, he saved me.

7 Return to your rest, my soul,
 for the LORD has been good to you.

8 For you, LORD, have delivered me from death,
 my eyes from tears,
 my feet from stumbling,
9 that I may walk before the LORD
 in the land of the living.

10 I trusted in the LORD when I said,
 "I am greatly afflicted";
11 in my alarm I said,
 "Everyone is a liar."

12 What shall I return to the LORD
 for all his goodness to me?

13 I will lift up the cup of salvation
 and call on the name of the LORD.
14 I will fulfill my vows to the LORD
 in the presence of all his people.

15 Precious in the sight of the LORD
 is the death of his faithful servants.
16 Truly I am your servant, LORD;
 I serve you just as my mother did;
 you have freed me from my chains.

17 I will sacrifice a thank offering to you
 and call on the name of the LORD.
18 I will fulfill my vows to the LORD
 in the presence of all his people,
19 in the courts of the house of the LORD —
 in your midst, Jerusalem.

Praise the LORD.[a]

---

[a] 19 Hebrew *Hallelu Yah*

Psalm 117

[1] Praise the LORD, all you nations;
　　extol him, all you peoples.
[2] For great is his love toward us,
　　and the faithfulness of the LORD endures forever.

　Praise the LORD.[a]

Psalm 118

[1] Give thanks to the LORD, for he is good;
　　his love endures forever.

[2] Let Israel say:
　　"His love endures forever."
[3] Let the house of Aaron say:
　　"His love endures forever."
[4] Let those who fear the LORD say:
　　"His love endures forever."

[5] When hard pressed, I cried to the LORD;
　　he brought me into a spacious place.
[6] The LORD is with me; I will not be afraid.
　　What can mere mortals do to me?
[7] The LORD is with me; he is my helper.
　　I look in triumph on my enemies.

[8] It is better to take refuge in the LORD
　　than to trust in humans.
[9] It is better to take refuge in the LORD
　　than to trust in princes.
[10] All the nations surrounded me,
　　but in the name of the LORD I cut them down.
[11] They surrounded me on every side,
　　but in the name of the LORD I cut them down.
[12] They swarmed around me like bees,
　　but they were consumed as quickly as burning thorns;
　　in the name of the LORD I cut them down.
[13] I was pushed back and about to fall,
　　but the LORD helped me.
[14] The LORD is my strength and my defense[b];
　　he has become my salvation.

[15] Shouts of joy and victory
　　resound in the tents of the righteous:
　"The LORD's right hand has done mighty things!
[16] 　The LORD's right hand is lifted high;
　　the LORD's right hand has done mighty things!"
[17] I will not die but live,
　　and will proclaim what the LORD has done.

---

[a] 2 Hebrew *Hallelu Yah*　　[b] 14 Or *song*

¹⁸ The Lᴏʀᴅ has chastened me severely,
    but he has not given me over to death.
¹⁹ Open for me the gates of the righteous;
    I will enter and give thanks to the Lᴏʀᴅ.
²⁰ This is the gate of the Lᴏʀᴅ
    through which the righteous may enter.
²¹ I will give you thanks, for you answered me;
    you have become my salvation.

²² The stone the builders rejected
    has become the cornerstone;
²³ the Lᴏʀᴅ has done this,
    and it is marvelous in our eyes.
²⁴ The Lᴏʀᴅ has done it this very day;
    let us rejoice today and be glad.

²⁵ Lᴏʀᴅ, save us!
    Lᴏʀᴅ, grant us success!

²⁶ Blessed is he who comes in the name of the Lᴏʀᴅ.
    From the house of the Lᴏʀᴅ we bless you.[a]
²⁷ The Lᴏʀᴅ is God,
    and he has made his light shine on us.
  With boughs in hand, join in the festal procession
    up[b] to the horns of the altar.

²⁸ You are my God, and I will praise you;
    you are my God, and I will exalt you.

²⁹ Give thanks to the Lᴏʀᴅ, for he is good;
    his love endures forever.

Psalm 119[c]

א Aleph

¹ Blessed are those whose ways are blameless,
    who walk according to the law of the Lᴏʀᴅ.
² Blessed are those who keep his statutes
    and seek him with all their heart —
³ they do no wrong
    but follow his ways.
⁴ You have laid down precepts
    that are to be fully obeyed.
⁵ Oh, that my ways were steadfast
    in obeying your decrees!
⁶ Then I would not be put to shame
    when I consider all your commands.
⁷ I will praise you with an upright heart
    as I learn your righteous laws.
⁸ I will obey your decrees;
    do not utterly forsake me.

---

[a] 26 The Hebrew is plural.   [b] 27 Or *Bind the festal sacrifice with ropes / and take it*   [c] This psalm is an acrostic poem, the stanzas of which begin with successive letters of the Hebrew alphabet; moreover, the verses of each stanza begin with the same letter of the Hebrew alphabet.

ב Beth

⁹ How can a young person stay on the path of purity?
　　By living according to your word.
¹⁰ I seek you with all my heart;
　　do not let me stray from your commands.
¹¹ I have hidden your word in my heart
　　that I might not sin against you.
¹² Praise be to you, LORD;
　　teach me your decrees.
¹³ With my lips I recount
　　all the laws that come from your mouth.
¹⁴ I rejoice in following your statutes
　　as one rejoices in great riches.
¹⁵ I meditate on your precepts
　　and consider your ways.
¹⁶ I delight in your decrees;
　　I will not neglect your word.

ג Gimel

¹⁷ Be good to your servant while I live,
　　that I may obey your word.
¹⁸ Open my eyes that I may see
　　wonderful things in your law.
¹⁹ I am a stranger on earth;
　　do not hide your commands from me.
²⁰ My soul is consumed with longing
　　for your laws at all times.
²¹ You rebuke the arrogant, who are accursed,
　　those who stray from your commands.
²² Remove from me their scorn and contempt,
　　for I keep your statutes.
²³ Though rulers sit together and slander me,
　　your servant will meditate on your decrees.
²⁴ Your statutes are my delight;
　　they are my counselors.

ד Daleth

²⁵ I am laid low in the dust;
　　preserve my life according to your word.
²⁶ I gave an account of my ways and you answered me;
　　teach me your decrees.
²⁷ Cause me to understand the way of your precepts,
　　that I may meditate on your wonderful deeds.
²⁸ My soul is weary with sorrow;
　　strengthen me according to your word.
²⁹ Keep me from deceitful ways;
　　be gracious to me and teach me your law.

Memorize Scripture

Live It!

Read Psalm 119:9–16. To hide God's Word in your heart (Psalm 119:11) means to memorize a verse and then to do what it says. Here are fun ways to memorize Bible verses with a friend.

1. Read the verse aloud, but leave out one word. Have your friend fill in the word you left out. Take turns reading the verse, and each time leave out a different word.

2. Each time you read the verse aloud leave out one more word. The first time, one word; the second time, two words; and so on. You or your friend can fill in the words that were left out.

Psalm 119:9-16

3. Write the Bible verse on two cards. Cut out each word, and scramble the pieces of each card separately. See who can put the words in the right order in the shortest time.

³⁰ I have chosen the way of faithfulness;
 I have set my heart on your laws.
³¹ I hold fast to your statutes, LORD;
 do not let me be put to shame.
³² I run in the path of your commands,
 for you have broadened my understanding.

ה He

³³ Teach me, LORD, the way of your decrees,
 that I may follow it to the end.ᵃ
³⁴ Give me understanding, so that I may keep your law
 and obey it with all my heart.
³⁵ Direct me in the path of your commands,
 for there I find delight.
³⁶ Turn my heart toward your statutes
 and not toward selfish gain.
³⁷ Turn my eyes away from worthless things;
 preserve my life according to your word.ᵇ
³⁸ Fulfill your promise to your servant,
 so that you may be feared.
³⁹ Take away the disgrace I dread,
 for your laws are good.
⁴⁰ How I long for your precepts!
 In your righteousness preserve my life.

ו Waw

⁴¹ May your unfailing love come to me, LORD,
 your salvation, according to your promise;
⁴² then I can answer anyone who taunts me,
 for I trust in your word.
⁴³ Never take your word of truth from my mouth,
 for I have put my hope in your laws.
⁴⁴ I will always obey your law,
 for ever and ever.
⁴⁵ I will walk about in freedom,
 for I have sought out your precepts.
⁴⁶ I will speak of your statutes before kings
 and will not be put to shame,
⁴⁷ for I delight in your commands
 because I love them.
⁴⁸ I reach out for your commands, which I love,
 that I may meditate on your decrees.

ז Zayin

⁴⁹ Remember your word to your servant,
 for you have given me hope.

ᵃ 33 Or *follow it for its reward* ᵇ 37 Two manuscripts of the Masoretic Text and Dead Sea Scrolls; most manuscripts of the Masoretic Text *life in your way*

⁵⁰ My comfort in my suffering is this:
   Your promise preserves my life.
⁵¹ The arrogant mock me unmercifully,
   but I do not turn from your law.
⁵² I remember, Lᴏʀᴅ, your ancient laws,
   and I find comfort in them.
⁵³ Indignation grips me because of the wicked,
   who have forsaken your law.
⁵⁴ Your decrees are the theme of my song
   wherever I lodge.
⁵⁵ In the night, Lᴏʀᴅ, I remember your name,
   that I may keep your law.
⁵⁶ This has been my practice:
   I obey your precepts.

ח Heth

⁵⁷ You are my portion, Lᴏʀᴅ;
   I have promised to obey your words.
⁵⁸ I have sought your face with all my heart;
   be gracious to me according to your promise.
⁵⁹ I have considered my ways
   and have turned my steps to your statutes.
⁶⁰ I will hasten and not delay
   to obey your commands.
⁶¹ Though the wicked bind me with ropes,
   I will not forget your law.
⁶² At midnight I rise to give you thanks
   for your righteous laws.
⁶³ I am a friend to all who fear you,
   to all who follow your precepts.
⁶⁴ The earth is filled with your love, Lᴏʀᴅ;
   teach me your decrees.

ט Teth

⁶⁵ Do good to your servant
   according to your word, Lᴏʀᴅ.
⁶⁶ Teach me knowledge and good judgment,
   for I trust your commands.
⁶⁷ Before I was afflicted I went astray,
   but now I obey your word.
⁶⁸ You are good, and what you do is good;
   teach me your decrees.
⁶⁹ Though the arrogant have smeared me with lies,
   I keep your precepts with all my heart.
⁷⁰ Their hearts are callous and unfeeling,
   but I delight in your law.
⁷¹ It was good for me to be afflicted
   so that I might learn your decrees.
⁷² The law from your mouth is more precious to me
   than thousands of pieces of silver and gold.

י Yodh

73 Your hands made me and formed me;
   give me understanding to learn your commands.
74 May those who fear you rejoice when they see me,
   for I have put my hope in your word.
75 I know, LORD, that your laws are righteous,
   and that in faithfulness you have afflicted me.
76 May your unfailing love be my comfort,
   according to your promise to your servant.
77 Let your compassion come to me that I may live,
   for your law is my delight.
78 May the arrogant be put to shame for wronging me without cause;
   but I will meditate on your precepts.
79 May those who fear you turn to me,
   those who understand your statutes.
80 May I wholeheartedly follow your decrees,
   that I may not be put to shame.

כ Kaph

81 My soul faints with longing for your salvation,
   but I have put my hope in your word.
82 My eyes fail, looking for your promise;
   I say, "When will you comfort me?"
83 Though I am like a wineskin in the smoke,
   I do not forget your decrees.
84 How long must your servant wait?
   When will you punish my persecutors?
85 The arrogant dig pits to trap me,
   contrary to your law.
86 All your commands are trustworthy;
   help me, for I am being persecuted without cause.
87 They almost wiped me from the earth,
   but I have not forsaken your precepts.
88 In your unfailing love preserve my life,
   that I may obey the statutes of your mouth.

ל Lamedh

89 Your word, LORD, is eternal;
   it stands firm in the heavens.
90 Your faithfulness continues through all generations;
   you established the earth, and it endures.
91 Your laws endure to this day,
   for all things serve you.
92 If your law had not been my delight,
   I would have perished in my affliction.
93 I will never forget your precepts,
   for by them you have preserved my life.

94 Save me, for I am yours;
    I have sought out your precepts.
95 The wicked are waiting to destroy me,
    but I will ponder your statutes.
96 To all perfection I see a limit,
    but your commands are boundless.

מ Mem

97 Oh, how I love your law!
    I meditate on it all day long.
98 Your commands are always with me
    and make me wiser than my enemies.
99 I have more insight than all my teachers,
    for I meditate on your statutes.
100 I have more understanding than the elders,
    for I obey your precepts.
101 I have kept my feet from every evil path
    so that I might obey your word.
102 I have not departed from your laws,
    for you yourself have taught me.
103 How sweet are your words to my taste,
    sweeter than honey to my mouth!
104 I gain understanding from your precepts;
    therefore I hate every wrong path.

נ Nun

105 Your word is a lamp for my feet,
    a light on my path.
106 I have taken an oath and confirmed it,
    that I will follow your righteous laws.
107 I have suffered much;
    preserve my life, Lord, according to your word.
108 Accept, Lord, the willing praise of my mouth,
    and teach me your laws.
109 Though I constantly take my life in my hands,
    I will not forget your law.
110 The wicked have set a snare for me,
    but I have not strayed from your precepts.
111 Your statutes are my heritage forever;
    they are the joy of my heart.
112 My heart is set on keeping your decrees
    to the very end.[a]

ס Samekh

113 I hate double-minded people,
    but I love your law.

_____

[a] 112 Or decrees / for their enduring reward

Life in Bible Times

What God Is Like

Psalm 119:97 says that God is the lawgiver. He gives us rules to live by, to keep us from doing wrong. God is good, and he shows us how to do good. The writer of this psalm loved God's rules, thought about them "all day long," and obeyed them.

114 You are my refuge and my shield;
    I have put my hope in your word.
115 Away from me, you evildoers,
    that I may keep the commands of my God!
116 Sustain me, my God, according to your promise, and I will live;
    do not let my hopes be dashed.
117 Uphold me, and I will be delivered;
    I will always have regard for your decrees.
118 You reject all who stray from your decrees,
    for their delusions come to nothing.
119 All the wicked of the earth you discard like dross;
    therefore I love your statutes.
120 My flesh trembles in fear of you;
    I stand in awe of your laws.

ע Ayin

121 I have done what is righteous and just;
    do not leave me to my oppressors.
122 Ensure your servant's well-being;
    do not let the arrogant oppress me.
123 My eyes fail, looking for your salvation,
    looking for your righteous promise.
124 Deal with your servant according to your love
    and teach me your decrees.
125 I am your servant; give me discernment
    that I may understand your statutes.
126 It is time for you to act, Lord;
    your law is being broken.
127 Because I love your commands
    more than gold, more than pure gold,
128 and because I consider all your precepts right,
    I hate every wrong path.

פ Pe

129 Your statutes are wonderful;
    therefore I obey them.
130 The unfolding of your words gives light;
    it gives understanding to the simple.
131 I open my mouth and pant,
    longing for your commands.
132 Turn to me and have mercy on me,
    as you always do to those who love your name.
133 Direct my footsteps according to your word;
    let no sin rule over me.
134 Redeem me from human oppression,
    that I may obey your precepts.
135 Make your face shine on your servant
    and teach me your decrees.
136 Streams of tears flow from my eyes,
    for your law is not obeyed.

צ Tsadhe

137 You are righteous, LORD,
  and your laws are right.
138 The statutes you have laid down are righteous;
  they are fully trustworthy.
139 My zeal wears me out,
  for my enemies ignore your words.
140 Your promises have been thoroughly tested,
  and your servant loves them.
141 Though I am lowly and despised,
  I do not forget your precepts.
142 Your righteousness is everlasting
  and your law is true.
143 Trouble and distress have come upon me,
  but your commands give me delight.
144 Your statutes are always righteous;
  give me understanding that I may live.

ק Qoph

145 I call with all my heart; answer me, LORD,
  and I will obey your decrees.
146 I call out to you; save me
  and I will keep your statutes.
147 I rise before dawn and cry for help;
  I have put my hope in your word.
148 My eyes stay open through the watches of the night,
  that I may meditate on your promises.
149 Hear my voice in accordance with your love;
  preserve my life, LORD, according to your laws.
150 Those who devise wicked schemes are near,
  but they are far from your law.
151 Yet you are near, LORD,
  and all your commands are true.
152 Long ago I learned from your statutes
  that you established them to last forever.

ר Resh

153 Look on my suffering and deliver me,
  for I have not forgotten your law.
154 Defend my cause and redeem me;
  preserve my life according to your promise.
155 Salvation is far from the wicked,
  for they do not seek out your decrees.
156 Your compassion, LORD, is great;
  preserve my life according to your laws.

¹⁵⁷ Many are the foes who persecute me,
　　but I have not turned from your statutes.
¹⁵⁸ I look on the faithless with loathing,
　　for they do not obey your word.
¹⁵⁹ See how I love your precepts;
　　preserve my life, LORD, in accordance with your love.
¹⁶⁰ All your words are true;
　　all your righteous laws are eternal.

ש Sin and Shin

¹⁶¹ Rulers persecute me without cause,
　　but my heart trembles at your word.
¹⁶² I rejoice in your promise
　　like one who finds great spoil.
¹⁶³ I hate and detest falsehood
　　but I love your law.
¹⁶⁴ Seven times a day I praise you
　　for your righteous laws.
¹⁶⁵ Great peace have those who love your law,
　　and nothing can make them stumble.
¹⁶⁶ I wait for your salvation, LORD,
　　and I follow your commands.
¹⁶⁷ I obey your statutes,
　　for I love them greatly.
¹⁶⁸ I obey your precepts and your statutes,
　　for all my ways are known to you.

ת Taw

¹⁶⁹ May my cry come before you, LORD;
　　give me understanding according to your word.
¹⁷⁰ May my supplication come before you;
　　deliver me according to your promise.
¹⁷¹ May my lips overflow with praise,
　　for you teach me your decrees.
¹⁷² May my tongue sing of your word,
　　for all your commands are righteous.
¹⁷³ May your hand be ready to help me,
　　for I have chosen your precepts.
¹⁷⁴ I long for your salvation, LORD,
　　and your law gives me delight.
¹⁷⁵ Let me live that I may praise you,
　　and may your laws sustain me.
¹⁷⁶ I have strayed like a lost sheep.
　　Seek your servant,
　　for I have not forgotten your commands.

Psalm 120

A song of ascents.

¹I call on the LORD in my distress,
   and he answers me.
²Save me, LORD,
   from lying lips
   and from deceitful tongues.

³What will he do to you,
   and what more besides,
   you deceitful tongue?
⁴He will punish you with a warrior's sharp arrows,
   with burning coals of the broom bush.

⁵Woe to me that I dwell in Meshek,
   that I live among the tents of Kedar!
⁶Too long have I lived
   among those who hate peace.
⁷I am for peace;
   but when I speak, they are for war.

Psalm 121

A song of ascents.

¹I lift up my eyes to the mountains —
   where does my help come from?
²My help comes from the LORD,
   the Maker of heaven and earth.

³He will not let your foot slip —
   he who watches over you will not slumber;
⁴indeed, he who watches over Israel
   will neither slumber nor sleep.

⁵The LORD watches over you —
   the LORD is your shade at your right hand;
⁶the sun will not harm you by day,
   nor the moon by night.

⁷The LORD will keep you from all harm —
   he will watch over your life;
⁸the LORD will watch over your coming and going
   both now and forevermore.

Psalm 122

A song of ascents. Of David.

¹I rejoiced with those who said to me,
   "Let us go to the house of the LORD."
²Our feet are standing
   in your gates, Jerusalem.

³ Jerusalem is built like a city
   that is closely compacted together.
⁴ That is where the tribes go up —
   the tribes of the LORD —
  to praise the name of the LORD
   according to the statute given to Israel.
⁵ There stand the thrones for judgment,
   the thrones of the house of David.

⁶ Pray for the peace of Jerusalem:
   "May those who love you be secure.
⁷ May there be peace within your walls
   and security within your citadels."
⁸ For the sake of my family and friends,
   I will say, "Peace be within you."
⁹ For the sake of the house of the LORD our God,
   I will seek your prosperity.

Psalm 123

A song of ascents.

¹ I lift up my eyes to you,
   to you who sit enthroned in heaven.
² As the eyes of slaves look to the hand of their master,
   as the eyes of a female slave look to the hand of her mistress,
  so our eyes look to the LORD our God,
   till he shows us his mercy.

³ Have mercy on us, LORD, have mercy on us,
   for we have endured no end of contempt.
⁴ We have endured no end
   of ridicule from the arrogant,
   of contempt from the proud.

Psalm 124

A song of ascents. Of David.

¹ If the LORD had not been on our side —
   let Israel say —
² if the LORD had not been on our side
   when people attacked us,
³ they would have swallowed us alive
   when their anger flared against us;
⁴ the flood would have engulfed us,
   the torrent would have swept over us,
⁵ the raging waters
   would have swept us away.

⁶Praise be to the LORD,
  who has not let us be torn by their teeth.
⁷We have escaped like a bird
  from the fowler's snare;
 the snare has been broken,
  and we have escaped.
⁸Our help is in the name of the LORD,
  the Maker of heaven and earth.

Psalm 125

A song of ascents.

¹Those who trust in the LORD are like Mount Zion,
  which cannot be shaken but endures forever.
²As the mountains surround Jerusalem,
  so the LORD surrounds his people
  both now and forevermore.

³The scepter of the wicked will not remain
  over the land allotted to the righteous,
 for then the righteous might use
  their hands to do evil.

⁴LORD, do good to those who are good,
  to those who are upright in heart.
⁵But those who turn to crooked ways
  the LORD will banish with the evildoers.

Peace be on Israel.

Psalm 126

A song of ascents.

¹When the LORD restored the fortunes ofᵃ Zion,
  we were like those who dreamed.ᵇ
²Our mouths were filled with laughter,
  our tongues with songs of joy.
 Then it was said among the nations,
  "The LORD has done great things for them."
³The LORD has done great things for us,
  and we are filled with joy.

⁴Restore our fortunes,ᶜ LORD,
  like streams in the Negev.
⁵Those who sow with tears
  will reap with songs of joy.
⁶Those who go out weeping,
  carrying seed to sow,
 will return with songs of joy,
  carrying sheaves with them.

ᵃ 1 Or *LORD brought back the captives to*   ᵇ 1 Or *those restored to health*   ᶜ 4 Or *Bring back our captives*

Psalm 127

A song of ascents. Of Solomon.

¹Unless the LORD builds the house,
　　the builders labor in vain.
　Unless the LORD watches over the city,
　　the guards stand watch in vain.
²In vain you rise early
　　and stay up late,
　toiling for food to eat —
　　for he grants sleep to*ᵃ* those he loves.

³Children are a heritage from the LORD,
　　offspring a reward from him.
⁴Like arrows in the hands of a warrior
　　are children born in one's youth.
⁵Blessed is the man
　　whose quiver is full of them.
　They will not be put to shame
　　when they contend with their opponents in court.

Psalm 128

A song of ascents.

¹Blessed are all who fear the LORD,
　　who walk in obedience to him.
²You will eat the fruit of your labor;
　　blessings and prosperity will be yours.
³Your wife will be like a fruitful vine
　　within your house;
　your children will be like olive shoots
　　around your table.
⁴Yes, this will be the blessing
　　for the man who fears the LORD.

⁵May the LORD bless you from Zion;
　　may you see the prosperity of Jerusalem
　　all the days of your life.
⁶May you live to see your children's children —
　　peace be on Israel.

Psalm 129

A song of ascents.

¹"They have greatly oppressed me from my youth,"
　　let Israel say;
²"they have greatly oppressed me from my youth,
　　but they have not gained the victory over me.

ᵃ 2 Or *eat —* / *for while they sleep he provides for*

³Plowmen have plowed my back
 and made their furrows long.
⁴But the LORD is righteous;
 he has cut me free from the cords of the wicked."

⁵May all who hate Zion
 be turned back in shame.
⁶May they be like grass on the roof,
 which withers before it can grow;
⁷a reaper cannot fill his hands with it,
 nor one who gathers fill his arms.
⁸May those who pass by not say to them,
 "The blessing of the LORD be on you;
 we bless you in the name of the LORD."

Psalm 130

A song of ascents.

¹Out of the depths I cry to you, LORD;
² Lord, hear my voice.
 Let your ears be attentive
 to my cry for mercy.

³If you, LORD, kept a record of sins,
 Lord, who could stand?
⁴But with you there is forgiveness,
 so that we can, with reverence, serve you.

⁵I wait for the LORD, my whole being waits,
 and in his word I put my hope.
⁶I wait for the Lord
 more than watchmen wait for the morning,
 more than watchmen wait for the morning.

⁷Israel, put your hope in the LORD,
 for with the LORD is unfailing love
 and with him is full redemption.
⁸He himself will redeem Israel
 from all their sins.

Psalm 131

A song of ascents. Of David.

¹My heart is not proud, LORD,
 my eyes are not haughty;
 I do not concern myself with great matters
 or things too wonderful for me.
²But I have calmed and quieted myself,
 I am like a weaned child with its mother;
 like a weaned child I am content.

³Israel, put your hope in the LORD
 both now and forevermore.

Psalm 132

A song of ascents.

¹LORD, remember David
    and all his self-denial.

²He swore an oath to the LORD,
    he made a vow to the Mighty One of Jacob:
³"I will not enter my house
    or go to my bed,
⁴I will allow no sleep to my eyes
    or slumber to my eyelids,
⁵till I find a place for the LORD,
    a dwelling for the Mighty One of Jacob."

⁶We heard it in Ephrathah,
    we came upon it in the fields of Jaar:ᵃ
⁷"Let us go to his dwelling place,
    let us worship at his footstool, saying,
⁸'Arise, LORD, and come to your resting place,
    you and the ark of your might.
⁹May your priests be clothed with your righteousness;
    may your faithful people sing for joy.'"

¹⁰For the sake of your servant David,
    do not reject your anointed one.

¹¹The LORD swore an oath to David,
    a sure oath he will not revoke:
  "One of your own descendants
    I will place on your throne.
¹²If your sons keep my covenant
    and the statutes I teach them,
  then their sons will sit
    on your throne for ever and ever."

¹³For the LORD has chosen Zion,
    he has desired it for his dwelling, saying,
¹⁴"This is my resting place for ever and ever;
    here I will sit enthroned, for I have desired it.
¹⁵I will bless her with abundant provisions;
    her poor I will satisfy with food.
¹⁶I will clothe her priests with salvation,
    and her faithful people will ever sing for joy.

¹⁷"Here I will make a hornᵇ grow for David
    and set up a lamp for my anointed one.
¹⁸I will clothe his enemies with shame,
    but his head will be adorned with a radiant crown."

ᵃ 6 Or *heard of it in Ephrathah, / we found it in the fields of Jearim.* (See 1 Chron. 13:5,6) (And no quotation marks around verses 7-9) ᵇ 17 *Horn* here symbolizes strong one, that is, king.

Psalm 133

A song of ascents. Of David.

¹How good and pleasant it is
  when God's people live together in unity!

²It is like precious oil poured on the head,
  running down on the beard,
 running down on Aaron's beard,
  down on the collar of his robe.
³It is as if the dew of Hermon
  were falling on Mount Zion.
 For there the LORD bestows his blessing,
  even life forevermore.

Psalm 134

A song of ascents.

¹Praise the LORD, all you servants of the LORD
  who minister by night in the house of the LORD.
²Lift up your hands in the sanctuary
  and praise the LORD.

³May the LORD bless you from Zion,
  he who is the Maker of heaven and earth.

Psalm 135

¹Praise the LORD.ᵃ

 Praise the name of the LORD;
  praise him, you servants of the LORD,
²you who minister in the house of the LORD,
  in the courts of the house of our God.

³Praise the LORD, for the LORD is good;
  sing praise to his name, for that is pleasant.
⁴For the LORD has chosen Jacob to be his own,
  Israel to be his treasured possession.

⁵I know that the LORD is great,
  that our Lord is greater than all gods.
⁶The LORD does whatever pleases him,
  in the heavens and on the earth,
  in the seas and all their depths.
⁷He makes clouds rise from the ends of the earth;
  he sends lightning with the rain
  and brings out the wind from his storehouses.

ᵃ 1 Hebrew *Hallelu Yah*; also in verses 3 and 21

Family Praise Fun

Read Psalm 135. It praises God for the many great things he had done for the Israelites.

For family fun at the table, take turns telling something great that God has done. Each person must think of something new. A person who can't think of anything in five seconds loses a turn. Write each person's answer below. Count and see how many great things your family can remember about God.

Psalm 135:1-21

_____

_____

_____

_____

_____

_____

_____

_____

_____

_____

_____

_____

_____

_____

_____

_____

_____

_____

_____

_____

⁸ He struck down the firstborn of Egypt,
    the firstborn of people and animals.
⁹ He sent his signs and wonders into your midst, Egypt,
    against Pharaoh and all his servants.
¹⁰ He struck down many nations
    and killed mighty kings —
¹¹ Sihon king of the Amorites,
    Og king of Bashan,
    and all the kings of Canaan —
¹² and he gave their land as an inheritance,
    an inheritance to his people Israel.

¹³ Your name, LORD, endures forever,
    your renown, LORD, through all generations.
¹⁴ For the LORD will vindicate his people
    and have compassion on his servants.

¹⁵ The idols of the nations are silver and gold,
    made by human hands.
¹⁶ They have mouths, but cannot speak,
    eyes, but cannot see.
¹⁷ They have ears, but cannot hear,
    nor is there breath in their mouths.
¹⁸ Those who make them will be like them,
    and so will all who trust in them.

¹⁹ All you Israelites, praise the LORD;
    house of Aaron, praise the LORD;
²⁰ house of Levi, praise the LORD;
    you who fear him, praise the LORD.
²¹ Praise be to the LORD from Zion,
    to him who dwells in Jerusalem.

Praise the LORD.

Psalm 136

¹ Give thanks to the LORD, for he is good.

His love endures forever.

² Give thanks to the God of gods.

His love endures forever.

³ Give thanks to the Lord of lords:

His love endures forever.

⁴ to him who alone does great wonders,

His love endures forever.

⁵ who by his understanding made the heavens,

His love endures forever.

⁶ who spread out the earth upon the waters,

His love endures forever.

⁷ who made the great lights —

His love endures forever.

8 the sun to govern the day,

His love endures forever.

9 the moon and stars to govern the night;

His love endures forever.

10 to him who struck down the firstborn of Egypt

His love endures forever.

11 and brought Israel out from among them

His love endures forever.

12 with a mighty hand and outstretched arm;

His love endures forever.

13 to him who divided the Red Sea*a* asunder

His love endures forever.

14 and brought Israel through the midst of it,

His love endures forever.

15 but swept Pharaoh and his army into the Red Sea;

His love endures forever.

16 to him who led his people through the wilderness;

His love endures forever.

17 to him who struck down great kings,

His love endures forever.

18 and killed mighty kings —

His love endures forever.

19 Sihon king of the Amorites

His love endures forever.

20 and Og king of Bashan —

His love endures forever.

21 and gave their land as an inheritance,

His love endures forever.

22 an inheritance to his servant Israel.

His love endures forever.

23 He remembered us in our low estate

His love endures forever.

24 and freed us from our enemies.

His love endures forever.

25 He gives food to every creature.

His love endures forever.

26 Give thanks to the God of heaven.

His love endures forever.

Psalm 137

1 By the rivers of Babylon we sat and wept
    when we remembered Zion.
2 There on the poplars
    we hung our harps,

a 13 Or the Sea of Reeds; also in verse 15

³ for there our captors asked us for songs,
   our tormentors demanded songs of joy;
   they said, "Sing us one of the songs of Zion!"

⁴ How can we sing the songs of the Lord
   while in a foreign land?
⁵ If I forget you, Jerusalem,
   may my right hand forget its skill.
⁶ May my tongue cling to the roof of my mouth
   if I do not remember you,
  if I do not consider Jerusalem
   my highest joy.

⁷ Remember, Lord, what the Edomites did
   on the day Jerusalem fell.
  "Tear it down," they cried,
   "tear it down to its foundations!"
⁸ Daughter Babylon, doomed to destruction,
   happy is the one who repays you
   according to what you have done to us.
⁹ Happy is the one who seizes your infants
   and dashes them against the rocks.

Psalm 138

Of David.

¹ I will praise you, Lord, with all my heart;
   before the "gods" I will sing your praise.
² I will bow down toward your holy temple
   and will praise your name
   for your unfailing love and your faithfulness,
  for you have so exalted your solemn decree
   that it surpasses your fame.
³ When I called, you answered me;
   you greatly emboldened me.

⁴ May all the kings of the earth praise you, Lord,
   when they hear what you have decreed.
⁵ May they sing of the ways of the Lord,
   for the glory of the Lord is great.

⁶ Though the Lord is exalted, he looks kindly on the lowly;
   though lofty, he sees them from afar.
⁷ Though I walk in the midst of trouble,
   you preserve my life.
  You stretch out your hand against the anger of my foes;
   with your right hand you save me.
⁸ The Lord will vindicate me;
   your love, Lord, endures forever—
   do not abandon the works of your hands.

Psalm 139

For the director of music. Of David. A psalm.

¹You have searched me, LORD,
　　and you know me.
²You know when I sit and when I rise;
　　you perceive my thoughts from afar.
³You discern my going out and my lying down;
　　you are familiar with all my ways.
⁴Before a word is on my tongue
　　you, LORD, know it completely.
⁵You hem me in behind and before,
　　and you lay your hand upon me.
⁶Such knowledge is too wonderful for me,
　　too lofty for me to attain.

⁷Where can I go from your Spirit?
　　Where can I flee from your presence?
⁸If I go up to the heavens, you are there;
　　if I make my bed in the depths, you are there.
⁹If I rise on the wings of the dawn,
　　if I settle on the far side of the sea,
¹⁰even there your hand will guide me,
　　your right hand will hold me fast.
¹¹If I say, "Surely the darkness will hide me
　　and the light become night around me,"
¹²even the darkness will not be dark to you;
　　the night will shine like the day,
　　for darkness is as light to you.

¹³For you created my inmost being;
　　you knit me together in my mother's womb.
¹⁴I praise you because I am fearfully and wonderfully made;
　　your works are wonderful,
　　I know that full well.
¹⁵My frame was not hidden from you
　　when I was made in the secret place,
　　when I was woven together in the depths of the earth.
¹⁶Your eyes saw my unformed body;
　　all the days ordained for me were written in your book
　　before one of them came to be.
¹⁷How precious to me are your thoughts,ᵃ God!
　　How vast is the sum of them!
¹⁸Were I to count them,
　　they would outnumber the grains of sand —
　　when I awake, I am still with you.

¹⁹If only you, God, would slay the wicked!
　　Away from me, you who are bloodthirsty!

ᵃ 17 Or *How amazing are your thoughts concerning me*

_____

_____

_____

_____

_____

_____

_____

_____

_____

_____

_____

_____

_____

_____

_____

_____

_____

_____

_____

Life in Bible Times

What God Is Like

Psalm 139:13 says that God knew David even before David was born. God made David and loved him and watched him grow. God knew you and watched over you before you were born, too. You are special to God because he made you.

20 They speak of you with evil intent;
　　your adversaries misuse your name.
21 Do I not hate those who hate you, LORD,
　　and abhor those who are in rebellion against you?
22 I have nothing but hatred for them;
　　I count them my enemies.
23 Search me, God, and know my heart;
　　test me and know my anxious thoughts.
24 See if there is any offensive way in me,
　　and lead me in the way everlasting.

Psalm 140[a]

For the director of music. A psalm of David.

1 Rescue me, LORD, from evildoers;
　　protect me from the violent,
2 who devise evil plans in their hearts
　　and stir up war every day.
3 They make their tongues as sharp as a serpent's;
　　the poison of vipers is on their lips.[b]

4 Keep me safe, LORD, from the hands of the wicked;
　　protect me from the violent,
　　who devise ways to trip my feet.
5 The arrogant have hidden a snare for me;
　　they have spread out the cords of their net
　　and have set traps for me along my path.

6 I say to the LORD, "You are my God."
　　Hear, LORD, my cry for mercy.
7 Sovereign LORD, my strong deliverer,
　　you shield my head in the day of battle.
8 Do not grant the wicked their desires, LORD;
　　do not let their plans succeed.

9 Those who surround me proudly rear their heads;
　　may the mischief of their lips engulf them.
10 May burning coals fall on them;
　　may they be thrown into the fire,
　　into miry pits, never to rise.
11 May slanderers not be established in the land;
　　may disaster hunt down the violent.

12 I know that the LORD secures justice for the poor
　　and upholds the cause of the needy.
13 Surely the righteous will praise your name,
　　and the upright will live in your presence.

---

[a] In Hebrew texts 140:1-13 is numbered 140:2-14.　　[b] 3 The Hebrew has *Selah* (a word of uncertain meaning) here and at the end of verses 5 and 8.

Psalm 141

A psalm of David.

¹I call to you, LORD, come quickly to me;
  hear me when I call to you.
²May my prayer be set before you like incense;
  may the lifting up of my hands be like the evening sacrifice.

³Set a guard over my mouth, LORD;
  keep watch over the door of my lips.
⁴Do not let my heart be drawn to what is evil
  so that I take part in wicked deeds
 along with those who are evildoers;
  do not let me eat their delicacies.

⁵Let a righteous man strike me — that is a kindness;
  let him rebuke me — that is oil on my head.
 My head will not refuse it,
  for my prayer will still be against the deeds of evildoers.

⁶Their rulers will be thrown down from the cliffs,
  and the wicked will learn that my words were well spoken.
⁷They will say, "As one plows and breaks up the earth,
  so our bones have been scattered at the mouth of the grave."

⁸But my eyes are fixed on you, Sovereign LORD;
  in you I take refuge — do not give me over to death.
⁹Keep me safe from the traps set by evildoers,
  from the snares they have laid for me.
¹⁰Let the wicked fall into their own nets,
  while I pass by in safety.

Psalm 142[a]

A maskil[b] of David. When he was in the cave. A prayer.

¹I cry aloud to the LORD;
  I lift up my voice to the LORD for mercy.
²I pour out before him my complaint;
  before him I tell my trouble.

³When my spirit grows faint within me,
  it is you who watch over my way.
 In the path where I walk
  people have hidden a snare for me.
⁴Look and see, there is no one at my right hand;
  no one is concerned for me.
 I have no refuge;
  no one cares for my life.

---

[a] In Hebrew texts 142:1-7 is numbered 142:2-8.   [b] Title: Probably a literary or musical term

⁵I cry to you, LORD;
   I say, "You are my refuge,
      my portion in the land of the living."

⁶Listen to my cry,
   for I am in desperate need;
 rescue me from those who pursue me,
   for they are too strong for me.
⁷Set me free from my prison,
   that I may praise your name.
 Then the righteous will gather about me
   because of your goodness to me.

Psalm 143

A psalm of David.

¹LORD, hear my prayer,
   listen to my cry for mercy;
 in your faithfulness and righteousness
   come to my relief.
²Do not bring your servant into judgment,
   for no one living is righteous before you.
³The enemy pursues me,
   he crushes me to the ground;
 he makes me dwell in the darkness
   like those long dead.
⁴So my spirit grows faint within me;
   my heart within me is dismayed.
⁵I remember the days of long ago;
   I meditate on all your works
   and consider what your hands have done.
⁶I spread out my hands to you;
   I thirst for you like a parched land.ᵃ

⁷Answer me quickly, LORD;
   my spirit fails.
 Do not hide your face from me
   or I will be like those who go down to the pit.
⁸Let the morning bring me word of your unfailing love,
   for I have put my trust in you.
 Show me the way I should go,
   for to you I entrust my life.
⁹Rescue me from my enemies, LORD,
   for I hide myself in you.
¹⁰Teach me to do your will,
   for you are my God;
 may your good Spirit
   lead me on level ground.

ᵃ 6 The Hebrew has *Selah* (a word of uncertain meaning) here.

[11] For your name's sake, LORD, preserve my life;
    in your righteousness, bring me out of trouble.
[12] In your unfailing love, silence my enemies;
    destroy all my foes,
    for I am your servant.

Psalm 144

Of David.

[1] Praise be to the LORD my Rock,
    who trains my hands for war,
    my fingers for battle.
[2] He is my loving God and my fortress,
    my stronghold and my deliverer,
  my shield, in whom I take refuge,
    who subdues peoples[a] under me.

[3] LORD, what are human beings that you care for them,
    mere mortals that you think of them?
[4] They are like a breath;
    their days are like a fleeting shadow.

[5] Part your heavens, LORD, and come down;
    touch the mountains, so that they smoke.
[6] Send forth lightning and scatter the enemy;
    shoot your arrows and rout them.
[7] Reach down your hand from on high;
    deliver me and rescue me
  from the mighty waters,
    from the hands of foreigners
[8] whose mouths are full of lies,
    whose right hands are deceitful.

[9] I will sing a new song to you, my God;
    on the ten-stringed lyre I will make music to you,
[10] to the One who gives victory to kings,
    who delivers his servant David.

  From the deadly sword [11] deliver me;
    rescue me from the hands of foreigners
  whose mouths are full of lies,
    whose right hands are deceitful.

[12] Then our sons in their youth
    will be like well-nurtured plants,
  and our daughters will be like pillars
    carved to adorn a palace.
[13] Our barns will be filled
    with every kind of provision.

---

[a] 2 Many manuscripts of the Masoretic Text, Dead Sea Scrolls, Aquila, Jerome and Syriac; most manuscripts of the Masoretic Text *subdues my people*

Our sheep will increase by thousands,
　　by tens of thousands in our fields;
14　our oxen will draw heavy loads.[a]
There will be no breaching of walls,
　　no going into captivity,
　　no cry of distress in our streets.
15 Blessed is the people of whom this is true;
　　blessed is the people whose God is the LORD.

Psalm 145[b]

A psalm of praise. Of David.

1 I will exalt you, my God the King;
　　I will praise your name for ever and ever.
2 Every day I will praise you
　　and extol your name for ever and ever.

3 Great is the LORD and most worthy of praise;
　　his greatness no one can fathom.
4 One generation commends your works to another;
　　they tell of your mighty acts.
5 They speak of the glorious splendor of your majesty —
　　and I will meditate on your wonderful works.[c]
6 They tell of the power of your awesome works —
　　and I will proclaim your great deeds.
7 They celebrate your abundant goodness
　　and joyfully sing of your righteousness.

8 The LORD is gracious and compassionate,
　　slow to anger and rich in love.

9 The LORD is good to all;
　　he has compassion on all he has made.
10 All your works praise you, LORD;
　　your faithful people extol you.
11 They tell of the glory of your kingdom
　　and speak of your might,
12 so that all people may know of your mighty acts
　　and the glorious splendor of your kingdom.
13 Your kingdom is an everlasting kingdom,
　　and your dominion endures through all generations.

The LORD is trustworthy in all he promises
　　and faithful in all he does.[d]
14 The LORD upholds all who fall
　　and lifts up all who are bowed down.

---

[a] 14 Or *our chieftains will be firmly established*　[b] This psalm is an acrostic poem, the verses of which (including verse 13b) begin with the successive letters of the Hebrew alphabet.　[c] 5 Dead Sea Scrolls and Syriac (see also Septuagint); Masoretic Text *On the glorious splendor of your majesty / and on your wonderful works I will meditate*　[d] 13 One manuscript of the Masoretic Text, Dead Sea Scrolls and Syriac (see also Septuagint); most manuscripts of the Masoretic Text do not have the last two lines of verse 13.

¹⁵The eyes of all look to you,
and you give them their food at the proper time.
¹⁶You open your hand
and satisfy the desires of every living thing.

¹⁷The LORD is righteous in all his ways
and faithful in all he does.
¹⁸The LORD is near to all who call on him,
to all who call on him in truth.
¹⁹He fulfills the desires of those who fear him;
he hears their cry and saves them.
²⁰The LORD watches over all who love him,
but all the wicked he will destroy.

²¹My mouth will speak in praise of the LORD.
Let every creature praise his holy name
for ever and ever.

Psalm 146

¹Praise the LORD.^a

Praise the LORD, my soul.

²I will praise the LORD all my life;
I will sing praise to my God as long as I live.
³Do not put your trust in princes,
in human beings, who cannot save.
⁴When their spirit departs, they return to the ground;
on that very day their plans come to nothing.
⁵Blessed are those whose help is the God of Jacob,
whose hope is in the LORD their God.

⁶He is the Maker of heaven and earth,
the sea, and everything in them —
he remains faithful forever.
⁷He upholds the cause of the oppressed
and gives food to the hungry.
The LORD sets prisoners free,
⁸   the LORD gives sight to the blind,
the LORD lifts up those who are bowed down,
the LORD loves the righteous.
⁹The LORD watches over the foreigner
and sustains the fatherless and the widow,
but he frustrates the ways of the wicked.

¹⁰The LORD reigns forever,
your God, O Zion, for all generations.

Praise the LORD.

^a 1 Hebrew *Hallelu Yah*; also in verse 10

Psalm 147

¹Praise the LORD.ᵃ

How good it is to sing praises to our God,
    how pleasant and fitting to praise him!

²The LORD builds up Jerusalem;
    he gathers the exiles of Israel.
³He heals the brokenhearted
    and binds up their wounds.
⁴He determines the number of the stars
    and calls them each by name.
⁵Great is our Lord and mighty in power;
    his understanding has no limit.
⁶The LORD sustains the humble
    but casts the wicked to the ground.

⁷Sing to the LORD with grateful praise;
    make music to our God on the harp.

⁸He covers the sky with clouds;
    he supplies the earth with rain
    and makes grass grow on the hills.
⁹He provides food for the cattle
    and for the young ravens when they call.

¹⁰His pleasure is not in the strength of the horse,
    nor his delight in the legs of the warrior;
¹¹the LORD delights in those who fear him,
    who put their hope in his unfailing love.

¹²Extol the LORD, Jerusalem;
    praise your God, Zion.

¹³He strengthens the bars of your gates
    and blesses your people within you.
¹⁴He grants peace to your borders
    and satisfies you with the finest of wheat.

¹⁵He sends his command to the earth;
    his word runs swiftly.
¹⁶He spreads the snow like wool
    and scatters the frost like ashes.
¹⁷He hurls down his hail like pebbles.
    Who can withstand his icy blast?
¹⁸He sends his word and melts them;
    he stirs up his breezes, and the waters flow.

ᵃ 1 Hebrew *Hallelu Yah*; also in verse 20

[19] He has revealed his word to Jacob,
   his laws and decrees to Israel.
[20] He has done this for no other nation;
   they do not know his laws.[a]

Praise the LORD.

Psalm 148

[1] Praise the LORD.[b]

Praise the LORD from the heavens;
   praise him in the heights above.
[2] Praise him, all his angels;
   praise him, all his heavenly hosts.
[3] Praise him, sun and moon;
   praise him, all you shining stars.
[4] Praise him, you highest heavens
   and you waters above the skies.

[5] Let them praise the name of the LORD,
   for at his command they were created,
[6] and he established them for ever and ever—
   he issued a decree that will never pass away.

[7] Praise the LORD from the earth,
   you great sea creatures and all ocean depths,
[8] lightning and hail, snow and clouds,
   stormy winds that do his bidding,
[9] you mountains and all hills,
   fruit trees and all cedars,
[10] wild animals and all cattle,
   small creatures and flying birds,
[11] kings of the earth and all nations,
   you princes and all rulers on earth,
[12] young men and women,
   old men and children.

[13] Let them praise the name of the LORD,
   for his name alone is exalted;
   his splendor is above the earth and the heavens.
[14] And he has raised up for his people a horn,[c]
   the praise of all his faithful servants,
   of Israel, the people close to his heart.

Praise the LORD.

[a] 20 Masoretic Text; Dead Sea Scrolls and Septuagint *nation; / he has not made his laws known to them*   [b] 1 Hebrew *Hallelu Yah*; also in verse 14   [c] 14 *Horn* here symbolizes strength.

Psalm 149

[1] Praise the LORD.[a]

Sing to the LORD a new song,
  his praise in the assembly of his faithful people.

[2] Let Israel rejoice in their Maker;
  let the people of Zion be glad in their King.
[3] Let them praise his name with dancing
  and make music to him with timbrel and harp.
[4] For the LORD takes delight in his people;
  he crowns the humble with victory.
[5] Let his faithful people rejoice in this honor
  and sing for joy on their beds.

[6] May the praise of God be in their mouths
  and a double-edged sword in their hands,
[7] to inflict vengeance on the nations
  and punishment on the peoples,
[8] to bind their kings with fetters,
  their nobles with shackles of iron,
[9] to carry out the sentence written against them —
  this is the glory of all his faithful people.

Praise the LORD.

Psalm 150

[1] Praise the LORD.[b]

Praise God in his sanctuary;
  praise him in his mighty heavens.
[2] Praise him for his acts of power;
  praise him for his surpassing greatness.
[3] Praise him with the sounding of the trumpet,
  praise him with the harp and lyre,
[4] praise him with timbrel and dancing,
  praise him with the strings and pipe,
[5] praise him with the clash of cymbals,
  praise him with resounding cymbals.

[6] Let everything that has breath praise the LORD.

Praise the LORD.

[a] 1 Hebrew *Hallelu Yah*; also in verse 9   [b] 1 Hebrew *Hallelu Yah*; also in verse 6

Life in Bible Times

Dancing

In Bible times a man and a woman did not dance together. Usually a group of men or a group of women danced. People danced at weddings to show happiness. They danced at great feasts held to worship the Lord. David danced and leaped for joy when God's ark entered Jerusalem (2 Samuel 6:14–16).

Weights and Measures

	Biblical Unit	Approximate American Equivalent	Approximate Metric Equivalent
Weights	talent (60 minas)	75 pounds	34 kilograms
	mina (50 shekels)	1 1/4 pounds	560 grams
	shekel (2 bekas)	2/5 ounce	11.5 grams
	pim (2/3 shekel)	1/4 ounce	7.8 grams
	beka (10 gerahs)	1/5 ounce	5.7 grams
	gerah	1/50 ounce	0.6 gram
	daric	1/3 ounce	8.4 grams
Length	cubit	18 inches	45 centimeters
	span	9 inches	23 centimeters
	handbreadth	3 inches	7.5 centimeters
	stadion (pl. stadia)	600 feet	183 meters
Capacity			
Dry Measure	cor [homer] (10 ephahs)	6 bushels	220 liters
	lethek (5 ephahs)	3 bushels	110 liters
	ephah (10 omers)	3/5 bushel	22 liters
	seah (1/3 ephah)	7 quarts	7.5 liters
	omer (1/10 ephah)	2 quarts	2 liters
	cab (1/18 ephah)	1 quart	1 liter
Liquid Measure	bath (1 ephah)	6 gallons	22 liters
	hin (1/6 bath)	1 gallon	3.8 liters
	log (1/72 bath)	1/3 quart	0.3 liter

The figures of the table are calculated on the basis of a shekel equaling 11.5 grams, a cubit equaling 18 inches and an ephah equaling 22 liters. The quart referred to is either a dry quart (slightly larger than a liter) or a liquid quart (slightly smaller than a liter), whichever is applicable. The ton referred to in the footnotes is the American ton of 2,000 pounds. These weights are calculated relative to the particular commodity involved. Accordingly, the same measure of capacity in the text may be converted into different weights in the footnotes.

This table is based upon the best available information, but it is not intended to be mathematically precise; like the measurement equivalents in the footnotes, it merely gives approximate amounts and distances. Weights and measures differed somewhat at various times and places in the ancient world. There is uncertainty particularly about the ephah and the bath; further discoveries may shed more light on these units of capacity.

Field Notes